A Dictionary of Bible Symbols

A Dictionary of Bible Symbols

Prepared by W. Stuart Owen
Revised and enlarged by P. A. Grist and R. Dowling

Grace Publications

GRACE PUBLICATIONS TRUST
139 Grosvenor Avenue
London N5 2NH
England

Joint Managing Editors:
  H. J. Appleby
  J. P. Arthur M.A.

© Grace Publications Trust 1992
First printed 1992

ISBN 0 946462 27 5

Distributed by
EVANGELICAL PRESS
12 Wooler Street
Darlington
Co. Durham DL1 1RQ
England

Printed in Great Britain at the Bath Press, Avon.

Cover design by Insight Ltd, Ipswich, Suffolk, IP1 5NP.

CONTENTS

Introduction: Part I

The figurative language of the Bible

The Bible has been written to teach us God's thoughts. But God's thoughts are too wonderful for us human beings fully to understand. So in the Bible God speaks to us in ordinary, everyday human words, to make his truth clear to us. We could say that in the Bible God has to draw for us 'pictures in words' to help us see more clearly the spiritual truths of his thoughts. For example, the Bible says that God is 'the Shepherd of his people'. This does not mean that God is a real shepherd who looks after real sheep. Instead, this 'picture in words' of a shepherd shows us something of what God is like. It describes his nature. He is a God who cares for his people, watches over them and leads them. There is a special name for this way of using words: we call these 'pictures in words' - 'figurative language'.

Why were the Bible writers inspired to use so much of this figurative language? There are three reasons:

1. Many of the things God intends us to know can only be explained to us in such picture language. We can only understand what heaven is like because the Bible describes heaven in terms of the precious and lasting things which we know about in this world. That which we have no experience of (i.e. heaven) is illustrated by word pictures from that which we do have experience of (i.e. this world). When the Lord Jesus

taught people about the kingdom of heaven, he used parables based on everyday events and the ordinary people listened to him gladly. They could see what Jesus meant because Jesus used earthly picture language, not a divine language the people could not understand (see Matthew 13:35).

2. Sometimes, though, the meaning of figurative language is not clear to us straight away. So this picture language requires us to think hard about what a passage means. As we think out the meaning of figurative language our attitudes and opinions may be changed by that knowledge and we will mature as Christians. See Proverbs 1:1-7; Romans 12:2; Hebrews 5:12-14.

3. So figurative language may hide the truth as well as make it clear: it hides the truth from the careless or proud and makes it clear to God's people who seek to know the mind of God. For example, God's way of salvation is for humble seekers. Proud, self-righteous people are not ready to learn about being saved. We need to understand that we deserve hell and that only our receiving God's free grace can save us (see Mark 10:15). To see the meaning of the figurative language in the Bible, we must be born again by the Holy Spirit and made willing to learn, by him. See Isaiah 6:9,10; Matthew 11:25,26; 13:10-17; John 3:3; Acts 28:23-27; 1 Corinthians 3:9-15.

There are several kinds of figurative language in the Bible. They are described by different names. These are the main ones:

1. **A METONYMY** is a subject represented by something that is connected with it. Examples:

'Grey hair' is connected with being old and therefore represents an elderly person (Leviticus 19:32, AV). (NIV gives the meaning as 'the aged').

'Mouth or tongue' are connected with speaking or commanding and those words may therefore be used to represent a saying or a command (Deuteronomy 8:3 - God does not have a mouth; Proverbs 12:19).

'Diadem or sceptre' represent sovereignty (Genesis 49:10; Ezekiel 21:26). (NIV has 'turban' for AV 'diadem').

So the meaning of these words when they are used figuratively can be known by understanding what the words are normally connected with.

2. **A SYNECDOCHE** is when a part of something is used to represent the whole of it, or a whole of something represents a part of it. Examples:

'All the world' - a whole, represents the Roman Empire - part of the world (Luke 2:1, AV). (NIV gives the meaning as 'entire Roman world').

'Man' - part of a group of men and women - stands for men and women as a group and sometimes for all humankind (Genesis 1:27).

3. **A SIMILE** is a comparison in which something is said to be 'like' or 'as' something else. Example:

In Psalm 1 the blessed man is said to be 'like a tree planted by streams of water', whilst the wicked are 'like the chaff which the wind blows away'.

4. **A METAPHOR** is a kind of comparison, too; but in this case something is said actually to be something else, not simply to be like it. Examples:

'Judah is a lion's whelp' (Genesis 49:9). (NIV has 'lion's cub'). 'The Lord is my Shepherd' (Psalm 23:1).

Metaphors are often used about God. For example, God is said to have human emotions (e.g. grief - Genesis 6:6). God is said to have parts of a body (e.g. the arm of the Lord - Psalm 44:3). Metaphors are so commonly used that we sometimes forget they are only 'picture language'. They are not to be understood in a literal (human) sense, though they nevertheless picture something that is real.

5. **A SYMBOL** is a common object which has come to have a certain recognized meaning. Examples:

A rainbow is a symbol of God's love and faithfulness (Genesis 9:13-16; Ezekiel 1:28; Revelation 4:3).

A horn is a symbol of strength or power (Psalm 75:10; 132:17; 1 Samuel 2:1; Daniel 7:7,8; Zechariah 1:18-21).

The dreams and visions recorded in the Bible contain many symbols. The book of Revelation is full of symbols which signify spiritual meanings.

6. **A TYPE** is any person or thing in some way providing a visual picture at an earlier time, representing something or someone yet to appear in a later time. It is a kind of prophetic picture. Examples:

Noah's flood was a type of Christian baptism (1 Peter 3:20,21).

Melchizedek was a type of Christ (Hebrews 7).

The history of the Israelites' journey to Canaan was a type of the experience of the Christian life (1 Corinthians 10:1-13).

The tabernacle and the sacrifices described in Exodus and Leviticus contain many types of the life and death of Christ and of the manner of our fellowship with him.

7. **A PERSONIFICATION** is things which are not alive being spoken of as if they were people. Example:

In Psalm 98:8 the writer calls on the world of natural creation to give honour to God like this:

'Let the rivers clap their hands;
Let the mountains sing together for joy'.

Other examples are found in Psalm 65:12; 93:3; Isaiah 55:12.

8. **A PARABLE** is like a simile, in which one thing is compared to another, but it is much fuller and longer. A parable is a story of something that could happen in real life but its real purpose is to teach some spiritual truth. Parables were one of Jesus' favourite ways of teaching the people during his earthly ministry (see Matthew 13).

9. **AN ALLEGORY** is an enlarged metaphor; it is like a metaphor, in which something is said to be something else, but it, too, is fuller and longer than a metaphor. An allegory is a story in which many truths are taught by various metaphors, whereas in a parable only one main truth is usually being taught. Unlike parables, allegories do not always make good sense as stories - though some allegories do, such as Galatians 4:21-31. Other examples of allegories are Psalm 80:8-15; Proverbs 5:3-5; Ecclesiastes 12:3-7; John 15:1-8; 1 Corinthians 3:10-15.

Introduction: Part II

How do we recognize figurative language?

In the Bible, figurative language is the hardest kind of language to understand. We must first see whether a passage should be understood in its plain, natural sense, or whether figurative language is being used. This is most important. Wrong ideas about Christianity, and also false teaching, can begin if we understand figurative language as though it is literal truth or if we understand natural language only in a figurative sense. For example, Roman Catholics understand the language about the body and blood of Christ in John 6:54 and elsewhere in its natural sense: they understand Jesus to mean his real physical body and actual blood. Other false teachers are guilty of the opposite error: they treat the real events which the Bible records as no more than spiritual picture language. For example, when the Bible tells us about the virgin birth, or miracles, or the resurrection, they say that this is figurative language and not a record of what really happened. Both errors deny the true meaning of what Christ achieved on the cross and such misunderstandings will lead people who accept them into serious error.

Yet even faithful Bible scholars do not always agree about which words or passages are in figurative language and which are to be understood in their natural sense. Often it is clear when language is figurative: when Jesus said to his disciples 'You are the salt of the earth', he clearly did not mean that they were real salt: this language is figurative. But does Isaiah 14:12-15 refer to Satan? Not every Bible scholar thinks so. Nor does every Bible scholar believe that the 'thousand years' of Revelation 20 is figurative language - a METAPHOR, in fact, for the gospel age. Some argue that a literal one thousand years is meant.

So how are we to decide if a Bible passage is in figurative language rather than natural language? One old rule of Bible interpretation says that we should always understand a passage in its plain, natural, everyday meaning, unless this leads to nonsense. But the best method is to follow good rules of biblical interpretation which we will suggest here. As we apply these rules to a passage of the Bible, it will become clear whether the passage should be understood in its natural sense or whether figurative language is being used.

The correct attitude to the Bible

God speaks to us and shows himself to us through the Bible. Therefore our relationship to God must first of all be right, if we are to understand his Word (John 10:26,27). Rules for understanding the Bible will be of no use to us if our spiritual attitude or behaviour is displeasing to God.

We should therefore always remember these facts:

1. There is no other book in all the world like the Bible. It alone is inspired by God. Therefore we should read the Bible reverently and humbly. The great and holy God in his mercy and grace is willing to speak to weak and sinful people through his Word. We must remember that God resists the proud but gives grace to the humble (1 Peter 5:5). Therefore, if there are Bible passages which seem to us not to make sense, we should not treat them as mistakes. Instead, we should admit how poor our understanding is and how much we need God's help to understand his Word.

2. The Bible is a spiritual book. We need the help of the Holy Spirit to understand it (1 Corinthians 2:10-16). We must pray for his help earnestly and fervently (Psalm 119:18; Jeremiah 33:3). We must try to find the spiritual teaching in any part of the

Bible. The whole Bible has teaching which is needed by believers today (Romans 15:4; 2 Timothy 3:16).

3. The Bible is complete. It contains all that we need to know about God and how God expects us to respond to him in love and obedience. The Bible itself often teaches us how to understand the Bible. Understanding the culture in which the Bible was written will also add to our understanding of the meaning of the Bible. So the more we study the Bible, and its origins, the better we will understand it. See Isaiah 8:20; 2 Timothy 3:14-17; 2 Peter 1:3,4.

4. The Bible is a practical book. We are not simply to understand what the Bible says: we must do what it tells us, in every part of life. God does not want his people to have a lot of Bible knowledge but still to remain selfish and greedy. If we are trying to obey the Bible teaching which we already understand, God will usually help us to understand the Bible even better. (Proverbs 4:18; Luke 19:26; John 7:17; James1:21,22).

Here are some rules for understanding the Bible, especially its figurative language:

1. We must understand, first of all, the plain, natural everyday meaning of the words used in the Bible. We must try to find out what the words meant to the people who first heard them. The Bible's figurative language comes from what the Bible writers themselves knew: the plants, animals, mountains, weather, and so on, of the Bible lands. The more we know about such things, the better we will understand our Bibles. It is useful to know about the languages in which the Bible was first written, for words carry with them certain connected ideas. In New Testament times, for example, a 'race' would bring to mind the scenes at Greek athletic games where runners would put aside their usual long, flowing clothes and, after the race, would take their seats to watch the remaining events. All these ideas lie behind the picture of the Christian life in Hebrews 12:1,2. Again, in the Old Testament, the prophets often used similar-sounding words to make their message more vivid. For example, in Jeremiah's vision (Jeremiah 1:11,12) the almond

branch is said to mean that the Lord is watching over his Word to make sure that it is fulfilled. The Hebrew words for 'almond' and 'watching' sound alike - 'shaqed' and 'shoqed'. We do not have to know the original Bible languages, however, in order to understand most of the Bible's figurative language. A good translation of the Bible and, if possible, an analytical concordance, will help us to understand most of the figurative language quite well.

2. Studying the message of each passage as a whole is the most important part of understanding the Bible. First, we need to find the main message or theme of the book or psalm. Then we will try to distinguish between the main teaching and the details of the Bible passage we are looking at. Figurative language is often used to emphasize the main teaching of a passage. Once we understand the main teaching, we can often see what the figurative language is meant to emphasize.

Often, too, there are words in the passage which show us how to understand its meaning. We are usually told when a passage is a PARABLE; SIMILES always begin with a phrase containing the words 'as' or 'like'. Poetry and prophecies about the future usually contain much figurative language. In Hebrew poetry an idea is stated once and then the same idea, or its opposite, follows in different words. Often the language of one of these pairs of statements is natural and the language of the other statement is figurative. Because the statements are either repetitions or opposites, we can work out the meaning of the figurative language. For example, Psalm 21:9 says:

'At the time of your appearing
    you will make them like a fiery oven.
In his wrath the LORD will swallow them up,
    and his fire will consume them'.

Here the statement 'In his wrath the LORD will swallow them up' is repeating the idea of 'you will make them like a fiery oven'. So we can understand that 'like a fiery oven' is a SIMILE for God's wrath.

We may have to search through the whole of a long passage for a clue to its meaning. For example, in John 6:48-68 where Jesus refers to his 'flesh' and 'blood' we find the clue in verse 63. In that verse Jesus says: 'The words I have spoken to you are spirit and are life.' The words 'flesh' and 'blood' are therefore to be understood as figurative language symbolic of spiritual life and do not have their straightforward, physical meanings. This example shows how important it is to study the entire Bible passage when trying to decide which words are figurative and what they mean.

3. Sometimes the passage as a whole gives us no help in deciding which language is figurative. In such a case, we must try to find another Bible passage where the same subject is presented more clearly. A clear, full explanation of a subject elsewhere in the Bible will help us to understand a passage on the same subject which is shorter and less clear. It is nearly always helpful to compare Bible passages which are about the same subject. For example, compare all the Gospel accounts of the parable of the sower and see how each Gospel has some detail that the other Gospels leave out.

The Bible tells us that the New Testament makes clear much that is not so clear in the Old Testament (see Ephesians 3:3-6; Colossians 1:26; 1 Peter 1:10-12). Therefore we should use the clear New Testament teachings in order to understand the figurative language of the Old Testament. Many of the Old Testament types are explained in the New Testament; and, by using New Testament examples, we can understand other Old Testament symbols for ourselves (see, for example, Matthew 12:29; 16:11,12; John 2:19-22; 1 Corinthians 9:9-11; 2 Corinthians 4:6; Colossians 2:16,17; Hebrews 7).

On the other hand, and especially in the case of SYMBOLS, some figurative language is best understood by studying the passages where such language first occurs. For example, many of the SYMBOLS in the book of Revelation are taken from the Old Testament.

We also need to remember that the same figurative language can sometimes be used to describe different things - even, in some cases, opposites (for example, compare 1 Peter 5:8 with Revelation 5:5; John 3:14 with 2 Corinthians 11:3; Revelation 5:6 with Revelation 13:11). The same figurative language does not always mean the same thing. Yet if in each case we study the whole Bible passage, it becomes quite clear what the figurative language means.

4. It is important to find out what kind of figurative language is being used in a Bible passage. Is it a TYPE or a METAPHOR, a PARABLE or an ALLEGORY, for instance? Some people treat the parable of the Good Samaritan as an ALLEGORY. In so doing they find supposed meanings in all the details: the inn is the church, the two coins stand for the two sacraments (baptism and the Lord's Supper), and so on. There may be many ways to apply the main lesson in a PARABLE, yet we do not believe that this is the way to understand the meaning. In this example, it was Jesus' intention to show who is our neighbour and how we are to love him.

5. We must always remember that any passage of the Bible has only one clear sense or meaning (though that meaning may apply to different circumstances in different ways). This one meaning is the sense which God intends us to understand. John Owen once said: 'If the Scripture has more than one meaning, it has no meaning at all.' If all the different interpretations of a Bible passage were correct, then nobody would be able to say which was right and which was wrong. The Bible would have no authority and believers would have no certainty about anything. We should be thankful that God speaks in the Bible directly and clearly.

This does not mean that a passage of Scripture can only be applied to one set of circumstances or one period of history. Often the same passage has many applications. Also, the one meaning of a Bible passage can be quite complex. For example, Noah's flood is said to be a TYPE both of baptism (1 Peter 3:21,22) and of the day of judgment (Luke 17:27). Yet the basic meaning of this TYPE is the same. Baptism symbolizes our being united with Christ in his death (Romans 6:3-5). We know that in his death, Jesus was bearing our judgment instead of us.

Noah's flood teaches us that all sin must be punished by God. Our sin was punished in Jesus' death. Either Jesus bore that punishment in our place, if we are united to him, or we must bear that punishment ourselves in hell for ever. The one meaning of the TYPE - judgment on sin - has several layers of application.

In the same way, a prophetic passage may have an actual, historical fulfilment which, in turn, is a TYPE of another fulfilment yet to come. In Matthew 24 Jesus prophesied the destruction of Jerusalem which took place in AD70. Yet that awful event is also a TYPE of the end of the world, which is yet to be fulfilled.

Even so, we must be careful not to force out of a passage meanings which God never intended. For example, the fig tree in Matthew 24:32,33 is clearly, if we study the whole passage, a SIMILE for the signs of the end of the world. There is nothing in this passage which allows us to go further and interpret this same fig tree as here meaning a SYMBOL of Israel.

6. We should always remember that figurative language has its own limitations. For example, TYPES are not in every detail like the realities they represent. Joseph can be said to typify Christ because, like Christ, he was betrayed by his own people, suffered humiliation, was given a place of great authority, graciously forgave his people and saved them from death. Yet, unlike Jesus, Joseph was a sinner. Moreover, Joseph did not willingly enter into his sufferings. So Joseph is not like Jesus Christ in every detail. Just as we do not look for a meaning for every detail of a PARABLE, so we should not expect any figurative language to tell us every detail about what it stands for: it can only help us to understand some of the truth, not the whole truth. It is important to remember this, especially when we are dealing with figurative language applied to God.

7. Even when any Old Testament incident does have some figurative significance, we must not overlook the fact that it also contains lessons which we are to learn arising from the incident itself. For example, we must never think that Joseph was only figurative of Christ in some way. We can learn much from a study of how Joseph behaved in his own circumstances.

8. Finally, we should always check our understanding of a Bible
   passage with the rest of the Bible. Any interpretation which
   contradicts the clear teaching of the Bible elsewhere must be
   rejected as false. No interpretation should be based on figurative
   language alone; for figurative language is used to illustrate
   truths that are taught in straightforward language either in the
   same Bible passage or elsewhere in the Bible.

If we are to be good teachers of God's Word we must understand
that our knowledge is limited. We cannot expect to know at once
everything that the Bible teaches. Every believer is given the
ability to understand the basic truths of the Bible. Yet there is
much in the Bible about which we cannot be quite sure, and much
which may be a total mystery to us. As we continue to pray and
study our Bibles, our understanding will grow. Our questions
will gradually be answered, and obscure passages will become
clearer to us (see Proverbs 4:18; Hebrews 6:1-3). Those whom
God has called to be preachers must be able to speak with true
conviction (see 1 Peter 4:11). If they do not, then their message
will have little effect in the minds of their hearers. Also,
preachers must understand the Bible so well that they can make
its teachings clear and simple enough for everyone to
understand. This means that we must make every effort to
understand the text or passage we preach from. We should avoid
preaching on parts of the Bible which God has not yet made plain
to us. Some passages of figurative language are especially hard
to understand. We need to handle God's Word rightly and not
be too quick to think we know exactly what it means. Being an
effective preacher means spending time in prayer and Bible
study (see Acts 6:4). We pray that this little book may help you
grow in your understanding of the Scriptures and in being
effective as servants of the Lord.

Notes on the limitations of this Dictionary

1. The Bible contains so very much figurative language that it has not been possible to include every use in this dictionary. We have concentrated on the figurative language that occurs most often or is, we believe, the most important.

2. In many cases the same word has a number of different figurative meanings. Sometimes these meanings overlap and the word in a particular verse could be placed under one or two meanings. In such cases we have given the reference under the meaning we think most suitable.

   N.B. Certain words may be used in Scripture, sometimes figuratively, sometimes not. For example, 'armour' (1 Samuel 17 [literal use], cf. Ephesians 6 [figurative use].). Regard, of course, is always to be had to the context (and see Introduction - Part II).

3. Where there are thirty or more references for a particular meaning, we have included only a selection of Bible references.

How to use this Dictionary

1. Read through both parts of the introduction. Try to understand the different kinds of figurative language used in the Bible.

2. Whenever you find a Bible passage that seems to be using figurative language, look in the dictionary to see if the word/s in your Bible passage are included.

3. Check carefully whether more than one meaning is suggested for your word/s and make sure you select the correct meaning for your Bible passage.

4. Because this dictionary is designed to be used with either the King James version or other versions of the English Bible, the precise word/s in your Bible passage may not be in the list of words explained, but a very similar word may be given.

   Example: The word 'world'

   i. Look in the dictionary.

   ii. Check meanings - ten are given.

   iii. Decide carefully which meaning applies to the Bible passage you are considering.

   NOTE THAT THE WORD 'WORLD' IS OFTEN USED WITHOUT THE MEANING OF EVERY LIVING PERSON.

   Remember that a word can be used either literally or figuratively. Every word needs to be understood according to its context.

Abbreviations used in this dictionary

Genesis	Gen.	Nahum	Nah.
Exodus	Ex.	Habakkuk	Hab.
Leviticus	Lev.	Zephaniah	Zeph.
Numbers	Num.	Haggai	Hag.
Deuteronomy	Deut.	Zechariah	Zech.
Joshua	Josh.	Malachi	Mal.
Judges	Judg.	Matthew	Matt.
Ruth	Ruth	Mark	Mk.
1 Samuel	1 Sam.	Luke	Lk.
2 Samuel	2 Sam.	John	Jn.
1 Kings	1 Ki.	Acts	Acts
2 Kings	2 Ki.	Romans	Rom.
1 Chronicles	1 Chr.	1 Corinthians	1 Cor.
2 Chronicles	2 Chr.	2 Corinthians	2 Cor.
Ezra	Ez.	Galatians	Gal.
Nehemiah	Neh.	Ephesians	Eph.
Esther	Esth.	Philippians	Phil.
Job	Job	Colossians	Col.
Psalms	Ps.	1 Thessalonians	1 Thess.
Proverbs	Pro.	2 Thessalonians	2 Thess.
Ecclesiastes	Ecc.	1 Timothy	1 Tim.
Song of Songs	Song.	2 Timothy	2 Tim.
Isaiah	Isa.	Titus	Tit.
Jeremiah	Jer.	Philemon	Phm.
Lamentations	Lam.	Hebrews	Heb.
Ezekiel	Ezek.	James	Jas.
Daniel	Dan.	1 Peter	1 Pet.
Hosea	Hos.	2 Peter	2 Pet.
Joel	Joel	1 John	1 Jn.
Amos	Amos	2 John	2 Jn.
Obadiah	Ob.	3 John	3 Jn.
Jonah	Jon.	Jude	Jude
Micah	Mic.	Revelation	Rev.

Authorised Version   AV   New International Version   NIV
cf. = Compare

A Dictionary of Bible Symbols

Figure	**Interpretation and references**
Aaron	As the high priest appointed by God, he is often (but not always) a TYPE of Christ. Ex.4:14, etc. Heb.5:4
Aaron's rod	The buds, fruits and flowers produced by the rod can be taken as SYMBOLIZING the good effects produced by God in the people of his choice bringing them new life. Num.17 Heb.9:4
Abaddon (Heb.) Apollyon (Greek)	Means 'Destroyer'. The SYMBOLIC name for the leader of the fallen angels, i.e. Satan. Rev.9:11
Abomination of Desolation	A TYPE of the attempt by the Antichrist to violate everything that is sacred. This will take place shortly before the Lord returns. The idea is derived from the action of Antiochus Epiphanes who desecrated the Jerusalem temple in

167BC, and is reinforced by the desecration of the temple by the Romans in AD70.
Dan.11:31; 12:11
Matt.24:15; Mark 13:14

Abyss   See under 'Pit(s)'

Adam   A TYPE of Christ. Adam was not only a private person but the original head and representative of the human race. When Adam sinned, we all became guilty 'in' him. Also, as human beings, we all inherit Adam's sinful nature and the death that was to be the punishment of his disobedience (cf. Gen.2:17). Jesus Christ is the head and representative of a new humanity - those who are 'in him' by faith-union. In him, believers are righteous before God. Furthermore, Jesus is the 'firstborn among many brothers' (Rom.8:29). Believers receive a new and holy nature through him and, when he comes again, a resurrection body.
Rom.5:12,14,18; 1 Cor.15:22,45

Adultery (ies)   Sometimes used as a METAPHOR for unfaithfulness to God by the worship of idols or of possessions or of pleasure, etc., appropriately so since in Old Testament times much idol worship involved physical adultery.
See also 'Fornication' and 'Harlot'.
Jer.3:8,9; Ezek.23:37; Hos. 2:2; 5:3
Jas.4:4

Air   Just as the air controls the movements of clouds and waves, etc. so too does Satan control the thoughts and ambitions of sinful people.
Eph.2:2

Affliction	See under 'Wounds'.
Altar	The different kinds of altar TYPIFY the different aspects of our Saviour's death.
i. the altar of earth	Some suggest that this speaks to us of the humanity of Jesus. The Son of God had to humble himself in becoming man, so that he could be a sin offering for us. Ex.20:24, etc.
ii. the altar of stone	The stones used to construct this altar were to be unhewn. In this God is showing us that no human skill or work is able to contribute anything to our salvation. Jesus alone could bear the terrible punishment for our sins. Ex.20:25, etc.
iii. the altar of bronze	This suggests the unyielding demands of God's justice. This altar is also called the altar of burnt offering. It was not enough for Jesus to suffer terrible agonies. Jesus had to die in order to satisfy the demands of God's holy law on our behalf. See also under 'Brass'. Ex.27:1,2, etc.
iv. the altar of gold	This suggests the preciousness of the death of Christ. This altar was also the altar of incense. See also under 'Incense'. Ex.30:1-10, etc.
v. altars to idols or false altars	These SYMBOLIZE the false religions of the world in which people worship gods of their own imaginations, e.g. 1 Kings 13:1-5; 18:26; 2 Kings 16:10

Amalek	The Amalekites TYPIFY the spiritual enemies of God's people in all ages. Ex.17; Num.24:20; Deut.25:17,19; Judg.5:14; 1 Sam.15:2-5; 28:18
Ambassador	This is a METAPHOR for one who has been sent by Christ to represent his kingdom in the world, i.e. preachers of the gospel. 2 Cor.5:20
Ancient of Days	God reveals himself to Daniel as a very wise and majestic person, and someone very suitable to be the judge of all the earth. Dan.7:9,13,22.
Anoint(ing)	This SYMBOLIZES the Holy Spirit's work in setting apart and in equipping people to serve God. In the Old Testament priests (e.g. Ex.30:30), prophets (1 Ki.19:16) and kings (1 Ki.1:34) were anointed with oil when they began their work. They TYPIFIED Jesus who is the anointed one. 'Anointed' is what Messiah or Christ means. Jesus was anointed with the Holy Spirit (Luke 4:18) to be our great prophet, priest and king. Also, all Christians are anointed by the Holy Spirit (2 Cor.1:21; 1 Jn 2:27) enabling them to be prophets, priests and kings (1 Pet.2:9). See also under 'Oil'. Ex.30:30; Lev.8:12
Ariel ('hearth of God')	See under 'City' or 'Jerusalem'. Isa.29:1-7; See Ezek. 43:15, 16
Ark i. of Noah	TYPIFIES the Lord Jesus Christ as the sole means of salvation from the wrath of God. Gen.6-8

	Matt.24:38; Lk.17:27; Heb.11:7; 1 Pet.3:20
ii. of the covenant	SYMBOLIZES God present in the midst of his people. See under 'Mercy seat'. Ex.25:10-22; 40:20; Num.10:33; Deut.10:2-5; Josh.3-4; 1 Sam.4:21, etc.
Arm	A METAPHOR for power. In many verses it is used for the saving power of God. It is also used for political or military power (e.g. 2 Chron.32:8; Ps.10:15, etc.) Ex.6:6; 15:16; Ps.44:3, etc.
Armageddon (Megiddo)	The SYMBOLIC scene of the final battle of this age when the powers of evil in the world seek to overcome the church, and in which Christ will be victorious. The SYMBOL probably derives its significance from the fact that many decisive battles were fought there: Judg.5:19; 2 Ki.23:29. Rev.16:16; cf. 17:14; 19:19; 20:9
Armour	A METAPHOR for the spiritual protection which Jesus gives us to use in our fight against Satan. Rom.13:12; 2 Cor.6:7*; Eph.6:11-13 [*NIV translates as 'weapon']
Arrows	A METAPHOR for any kind of serious attack. Sometimes used of the attacks of the wicked against the righteous. Sometimes used for God's judgments on the ungodly. Deut.32:23,42; 2 Sam.22:15; Job 6:4; Ps.7:13; 11:2, etc.

Atonement cover	See 'Mercy seat'.

Babylon

A SYMBOL, in New Testament times, of Rome which like Babylon in Mesapotamia in Old Testament times was the political and religious capital of a world empire, emanating luxury and moral corruption. More broadly, it is a SYMBOL for the godless world-system which in every age entices and allures people away from Christ by offering them the temporary pleasures of sin.
1 Pet.5:13; Rev.14:8; 16:19; 17:5
cf. Is.21:9

Balance

A METAPHOR for the measurement of things generally. Sometimes for material things such as mountains; or for immaterial things such as sufferings. Sometimes it is used to refer to how one measures up to God's standards of righteousness.
Job 6:2*; 31:6*; Ps.62:9; Isa.40:12,15*
Dan. 5:27
[*NIV translates as 'scales']

Baptism
i. John's

A SYMBOL for turning away from sin to righteousness, i.e. repentance.
Matt.3:7; 21:25; Mk.1:4; 11:30;
Lk.3:3; 7:29; 20:4; Acts 1:22

ii. Christian

The SYMBOL for Christian conversion. That is, of death to sin and of new life in Christ.
Matt.28:19; Rom.6:4; Gal.3:27; Col.2:12

iii. Holy Spirit

a. The METAPHOR for the disciples being empowered at Pentecost. The emphasis, as with water baptism, is on initiation - the

	initiation of the church age (or age of the new covenant). Matt.3:11; Acts 1:5; 11:16
b.	The METAPHOR for a Christian actually receiving the Holy Spirit at conversion. The emphasis is again on initiation - the initiation of the individual Christian into the once-for-all event of Pentecost. 1 Cor.12:13, etc.

iv. Of suffering

A METAPHOR for one's being deeply immersed in sufferings. Especially used of Jesus' suffering the agonies of the cross.
Mk.10:38; Lk.12:50

Bear

A SYMBOL of worldly power, suggestive of ferocity and cunning.
Dan.7:5
Rev.13:2

Beast
i. From the sea/ abyss

A SYMBOL of the human instruments, whether nations or governments, used by Satan to persecute God's people.
Rev.13:1-10 (cf Dan.7); Rev.11:7; 15:2; 17:8,11,12; 19:19; 20:10

ii. From the earth

A SYMBOL of the false religions and philosophies of the world.
Rev.13:11-18; 16:13

iii. Brute (wild)

A SYMBOL for people who are ungodly, cruel and heathen.
1 Cor.15:32; Titus 1:12;
2 Pet.2:12; Jude 10
[NIV 'unreasoning' animals]

Beasts

See 'Living creatures'.
cf. Rev.4-7

Beat oft	See under 'Thresh(ing)'.

Belial

i.   A name of Satan meaning 'worthless' or 'ungodly'.
2 Cor.6:15

ii.   Children of Belial - a METAPHOR for unbelievers who reflect the character of Satan in their lives.
Deut.13:13; Judg.20:13;
1 Sam.10:27; 1 Ki.21:13
[NIV translates as 'wicked men or 'troublemakers' or 'scoundrels'].

Bethshemesh   See under 'Sun'.

Bitter   See under 'Sour'.

Bitterness   See under 'Gall'.

Black, Blackness

The SYMBOLIC colour of judgment and death.
See also 'Dark(ness)' and 'Sackcloth'.
Zech.6:2,6;
Jude 13; Rev.6:5,12

Block(ed)   See under 'Hedge(d)'.

Blood

i.   A METONYMY for the life of a creature, especially life violently forfeited (as in animal sacrifices). The sprinkling of the blood of the Old Testament sacrifices TYPIFIED the cleansing from our sins through the death of Christ.
Gen.9:4-6; Lev.17:11; Deut.12:23
Heb.9:7-25

ii.   A SYMBOL for the defilement of sin.
Lev.20:18 [AV only]; Ezek.16:6-22

Blow   See under 'Wound'.

Blue   The blue thread used in the veil of both
                        the tabernacle and the temple is thought
                        by some to SYMBOLIZE the heavenly
                        origin of Christ (as the sky is blue).
                        See under 'Veil (iii)'.
                        Ex.25:4; 26:1; Num.4:6-11;
                        2 Chron.2:7,14, etc.

Body   One of the METAPHORS used to
                        describe the church. Under the headship
                        of Christ, the church is a living unity, like
                        a body, with each member in organic
                        relationship with all the other members.
                        Rom.12:4,5; 1 Cor.10:16,17; 12:12-27;
                        Eph.1:23; 2:16; 3:6; 4:4-16; 5:23,30;
                        Col.1:18; 2:19

Book(s)   SYMBOLICALLY used to describe the
                        record which God keeps of all the details
                        of our lives. One special book, often
                        called 'The Book of Life', refers to the
                        record kept in heaven of the names of
                        God's elect.
                        See also under 'Scroll'.
                        Ex.32:32,33; Ps.56:8; 69:28; 139:16;
                        Dan.12:1; Mal.3:16;
                        Phil.4:3; Rev.3:5; 5:1; 13:8; 17:8;
                        20:12,15; 21:27; 22:19
                        See also Luke 10:20.

Book of life   See under 'Book(s)' and 'Tree of life'.

Bottles   See under 'Wineskin(s)'.

Bough   See under 'Vine(s)'.

Bramble   See under 'Thorn(s)'.

Branch   One of the titles of Christ. Sometimes
                       showing his divine nature - 'the Branch
                       of the Lord', and sometimes his human
                       nature - '..unto David a righteous Branch'.
                       Isa.4:2; 11:1; Jer.23:5; 33:15;
                       Zech.3:8; 6:12

Brass/Bronze   A metal which is often used to
                       SYMBOLIZE judgment, especially
                       God's judgment.   In Old Testament
                       times the metal was probably a mixture
                       of copper and tin, which we would call
                       bronze.
                       Ex.27:2-6; Lev.26:19;
                       Rev.1:15, etc.

Breach   See under 'Wound(s)'.

Bread   The 'bread from heaven' of the exodus is
                       a TYPE of Christ. Similarly the bread of
                       the communion service SYMBOLIZES
                       the body of Christ. Both figures teach the
                       same lesson, i.e. that Christ is the only
                       proper nourishment our souls need.
                       See also under 'Manna'.
                       Ex.16:4-32; Neh.9:15;
                       Lk.22:19; Jn.6:31-48; 1 Cor.10:16,17;
                       11:23, etc.

Bride   A METAPHOR for the church, i.e. those
                       who are joined by faith to Christ in an
                       eternal bond of love.
                       See also under 'Wife', Eph.5:25-33.
                       Isa.62:5;
                       Jn.3:29; Rev.21:2,9; 22:17

Bridegroom   A METAPHOR for Christ showing his
                       great love and faithfulness towards his
                       people.
                       Isa.62:5;
                       Matt.9:15; 25:1-10; Mk.2:19,20;
                       Lk.5:34,35; Jn.3:29

Briers	See under 'Thistle(s)'.
Bright	See under 'Shine(s)'.
Brimstone/Sulphur	A SYMBOL for wrath, especially the wrath of God. Gen.19:24; Deut.29:23; Job 18:15; Ps.11:6; Isa.30:33; 34:9; Ezek.38:22; Lk.17:29; Rev.9:17,18; 14:10; 19:20; 20:10; 21:8
Bronze	See under 'Brass'.
Build, Building	Often used as a METAPHOR for the church, to describe its structure and its organization, together with the integration of all the members. Matt.16:18; 1 Cor.3:9,10; Eph.2:22 (cf. 1 Pet.2:5)
Buckler	See under 'Shield'.
Burdens	See under 'Yoke'.
Calloused	See under 'Fat(ness)'.
Canals	See under 'River(s)'.
Candle, Candlestick	See under 'Lamp/Lampstand'.
Capstone	See under 'Corner-stone'.
Cattle	See under 'Sheep'.
Cedar	Often used as a METAPHOR for greatness and majesty. Sometimes also denoting human pride. See also under 'Tree'. Judg.9;15; Job 40:17; Ps.29:5; 92:12; Song.1:17; 5:15; 8:9;

Isa.2:13; 14:8; 37:24; 41:19;
Jer.22:7,23; Ezek.31:8; Amos 2:9;
Zech.11:1,2

Chaff

A SYMBOL used to describe the
character of the wicked. Like chaff, the
wicked are worthless in God's sight.
Job 21:18; Ps.1:4; 35:5; Isa.5:24*;
17:13; 29:5; 33:11; 41:15; Jer.23:28+;
Dan.2:35; Hos.13:3; Zeph.2:2
Matt.3:12; Lk.3:17
[*NIV translates as 'Dry grass';
+NIV translates as 'Straw']

Chariot

i.   A SYMBOL of military might.
        Gen.41:43, etc.

ii.   A METAPHOR for God's mighty
        army of angels.
        2 Ki.2:11,12; 13:14; Ps.68:17

iii.   A SIMILE for the power of
        the fallen angels.
        Rev.9:9

Child, Children

i.   A SIMILE for the trusting and
        dependent attitude needed to come
        to Christ and to enter his kingdom.
        Matt.18:2-5; 19:13; Mk.9:36,37;
        10:15; Lk.9:47; 18:17

ii.   Children of God or of the kingdom
        or of the Father. A METAPHOR
        for those who have been born
        again of the Holy Spirit and who
        reflect God's character in their
        lives.
        See also under 'Son(s)'.
        Deut.14:1
        Matt.5:45*; Lk.6:35*; Jn.1:12
        Eph.5:1; 1 Jn.3:1,2,10
        [*NIV translates as 'son']

Circumcision	i.	A SYMBOL for true repentance which is a radical break with sin. Rom.2:28,29; Col.2:11, etc.
	ii.	A METAPHOR for the Jews who were zealous for the outward observance of the laws of Moses. Rom.4:9; Gal.2:9*; Tit.1:10, etc. [*NIV translates as 'to the Jews']

Cisterns   A METAPHOR for all the different ways people try to find true satisfaction other than in God.
Jer.2:13

City of refuge   A TYPE of Christ, the only secure refuge for sinners from the condemnation of the law.
Num.35:25-32; Josh.21:13-38

City of God,
Holy City, etc.   In the Old Testament, Jerusalem or Zion TYPIFIED the church. In the New Testament also it is used as a METAPHOR for the people of God, especially as they will be in glory.
See also under 'Jerusalem' and 'Zion'.
Ps.46:4; 48:1,8; 87:3; Isa.48:2; 52:1
Heb.12:22; Rev.3:12; 21:2; 22:19, etc.

Clean, Cleanse   A METAPHOR for the removal of sin and for being made holy.
See also under 'Wash'.
Gen.7:2; Lev.16:19;
1 Jn.1:9*, etc.
[*NIV translates as 'purify']

Cloak   See under 'Garment'.

Cloth(es,ing)   See under 'Garment'.

Cloud(s)   i.   A SYMBOL associated with
                          God's judgments.
                          Gen.9:13; Ex.14:20; 19:16;
                          Isa.19:1; Lam.3:44; Ezek.1:4
                          Joel 2:2;
                          Lk.21:27; Rev.14:14-16, etc.

                  ii.   Sometimes used as a SYMBOL
                          for a large number or a great
                          multitude.
                          Isa.44:22;
                          Heb.12:1
                          See also under 'Pillar of cloud'
                          and 'Smoke'.

Consume   See under 'Eat(ing)'.

Corner-stone   A SYMBOL for Christ who holds the
                          church together as the corner-stone of a
                          building holds its walls together.
                          See also under 'Foundation'.
                          Ps.118:22*; Isa.28:16;
                          Eph.2:20; 1 Pet.2:6
                          [*NIV translates as 'capstone']

Cornfloor   See under 'Thresh(ing)'.

Countries   See under 'World'.

Cover, Covering   i.   A METAPHOR for protection or
                          defence, particularly by God for
                          his people.
                          Ex.33:22; Deut.33:12*; Ps.91:4;
                          140:7; Isa.51:16
                          [*NIV translates as 'shield']

                  ii.   A METAPHOR for the pardon
                          and forgiveness of sins.
                          Ps.32:1; 85:2
                          Rom.4:7

                          See also under 'Mercy seat'.

Crop	See under 'Fruit(s)'.

Cross

Sometimes used as a METAPHOR for the painful trials sent to test our faith.
Matt.10:38; 16:24; Mk.8:34;
10:21 [AV only]; Lk.9:23; 14:27

Crown

i.   A SYMBOL for sovereignty and power.
2 Ki.11:12; Esther 2:17, etc.
Song.3:11

ii.   A SYMBOL for honour or victory.
Ex.25:11 [AV only]; Pr.4:9;
16:31; Isa.62:3;
Phil.4:1; Heb.2:9, etc.

iii.   A SYMBOL for the richness of God's grace towards his people.
Ps.65:11; 103:4; Isa 28:5;
Ezek.16:12
James 1:12; 1 Pet.5:4; Rev.2:10;
3:11

Crucified

Sometimes used as a METAPHOR to describe a believer's being delivered from the power of sin and of Satan through the cross of Christ.
Rom.6:6; Gal.2:20; 5:24; 6:14

Crystal

A SYMBOL for purity and holiness.
Rev.4:6; 21:11; 22:1

Cup

i.   A METAPHOR for the judgments of God.
Ps.75:8; Isa.51:17,22;
Jer.25:15,17,28; 49:12; 51:7;
Lam.4:21; Ezek.23:31; Hab.2:16;
Zech.12:2;
Rev.14:10; 16:19; 18:6

ii.	A METAPHOR for the blessings of God. Ps.16:5; 23:5
iii.	A METAPHOR for the deceptive pleasures of sin. Rev.17:4
iv.	A METAPHOR for suffering for righteousness' sake, especially applied to the sufferings of our Lord. Matt.20:22,23; 26:39,42; Mk.10:38,39; 14:36; Lk.22:42; Jn.18:11
v.	A METONYMY for the wine of the Lord's Supper. Lk.22:20; 1 Cor.10:16; 11:25,26

Currents   See under 'Flood'.

Curtain   See under 'Tent,ii', and 'Veil,i'.

Dark, Darkness,   i.   A METAPHOR for obscurity or
Darkly   mysteriousness.

i.	A METAPHOR for obscurity or mysteriousness. Num.12:8*; 1 Ki.8:12; Job 38:2; Ps.49:4*; 78:2+; Pro.1:6*; Isa.45:19; Dan.2:22; 1 Cor.13:12 [AV only] [*NIV translates as 'riddles'; +NIV translates as 'hidden']
ii.	A METAPHOR for the place of misery and punishment, finding its ultimate expression in hell. Ps.143:3; Isa.59:9; Jer.13:16; Lam.3:6; Matt.8:12; 22:13; 25:30; Jude 6,13

iii. A SYMBOL of judgment, especially God's judgment. Ex.10:15*,21; Deut.4:11; Ps.105:28; Pro.20:20; Isa.5:30; Ezek.32:8; Joel 2:2; Amos 5:18; Acts 2:20; Rev.8:12; 9:2; 16:10 [*NIV translates as 'black']

iv. A METAPHOR for the spiritual ignorance and blindness produced by sin. Ps.69:23; 82:5; Pro.2:13; Isa.9:2; 29:15; 42:7; 60:2; Jn.1:5; 3:19; 8:12; Eph.6:12; 1 Thess.5:4; 1 Jn.1:6

v. A SYMBOL of a believer's lack of a sense of God's presence. Job 30:26; Ps.88:6; Isa.50:10

David   One of the most important TYPES of Christ in the Old Testament, especially pointing to Christ as both the king and shepherd of his people. Isa.9:7; 55:3; Jer.30:9; Ezek.34:23; 37:24; Amos 9:11, etc.

Day   Often used as a METAPHOR for a definite time, e.g. 'day of the Lord', 'days of Noah', 'day of judgment', etc. Isa.13:6; Jer.30:7; Hos.1:11; Joel 2:11,31; Mal.4:5; Matt.12:36; 2 Pet.3:7, etc.

Day and Night   A METAPHOR for something lasting or that which is continually repeated. Josh.1:8; Ps.32:4; Isa.27:3; Mk.5:5; Acts 26:7; 2 Thess.3:8; 2 Tim.1:3; Rev.7:15, etc.

Dayspring	See under 'Sun'.

Dead

i.   A METAPHOR for those who are spiritually dead, i.e. unbelievers. Jn.5:25; Rom.4:17; Eph.2:1; 5:14; Col.2:13; etc.

ii.   A METAPHOR for a believer's not being under the power of sin. Rom.6:2*,11; 8:10; Gal.2:19*; Col.2:20*
[*NIV translates as 'died']

iii. A METAPHOR for weakness or impotence. 1 Sam.24:14; Rom.4:19; Heb.11:12; Rev.1:17

iv.   A METAPHOR for the corruption of sin. Matt.23:27; Heb.6:1*; 9:14
[*NIV translates as 'death']

Death

Physical death is both God's punishment on sin and a SYMBOL of lack of spiritual life. First of all there is spiritual death in this life. Then there is spiritual separation and punishment after physical death. Finally, after the resurrection, there will be the 'second death' in which Satan and all the wicked will suffer punishment for ever.
See also under 'Dead'.
Ps.56:13; Pro.2:18; 5:5; 14:12; Jn.5:24; 8:51; Rom.6:21,23; 8:2,6; James 1:15; 5:20; Rev.20:6, etc.

Defiled	See under 'Unclean'.
Devour	See under 'Eat(ing)'.

Dew		Sometimes used as a METAPHOR for a refreshing blessing from God which renews one's strength. Gen.27:28; Deut.32:2; 33:13; Ps.110:3; 133:3; Hos.14:5
Dirt		See under 'Mire'.
Dog	i.	A METAPHOR for the enemies of God's people. Dogs in the East are often vicious and live by scavenging in garbage. The Jews sometimes applied the term to Gentiles. Paul (Phil.3) applied the term to Judaizers - Jewish professing Christians who were undermining the gospel and the church. Ps.22:16,20; Pro.26:11; Matt.7:6; Phil.3:2; 2 Pet.2:22; Rev.22:15, etc.
	ii.	A term of insult against others or of humility when used of oneself. 1 Sam.17:43; 24:14; 2 Sam.3:8; 9:8; 16:9; 2 Ki.8:13; Matt.15:27; Mk.7:28, etc.
Door	i.	A METAPHOR for the way whereby sinners may be reconciled to God. Hos.2:15; Jn.10:1-9*; Acts 14:27 [*NIV translates as 'gate']
	ii.	A METAPHOR for an opportunity to declare the gospel. 1 Cor.16:9; 2 Cor.2:12; Col,4:3; Rev.3:8

	iii.	A METAPHOR for the second coming of Christ. Matt.24:33; Mk.13:29; James 5:9

	iv.	A METAPHOR for the way of obedience leading to the believer's enjoyment of the presence of Christ. See also under 'Gate'. Rev.3:20

Dove i. A METAPHOR or SIMILE used to describe the gentle and inoffensive nature given to believers in Christ.
Ps.74:19; Song.2:14; 5:2; 6:9; Isa.60:8; Hos.11:11; Matt.10:16

ii. The doves used in the Old Testament sacrifices were TYPICAL of Christ.
Lev.12:6; 14:22; Lk.2:24

iii. A SYMBOL of the Holy Spirit. Again suggesting his pure, gentle and sensitive nature.
Matt.3:16; Mk.1:10; Lk.3:22 Jn.1:32

iv. A METONYMY for mourning. The cooing of doves resembles the sounds of people expressing their grief.
Isa.38:14; 59:11; Ezek.7:16; Nahum 2:7

Dragon A SYMBOL for Satan, suggesting his ferocity, power and cunning.

Isa.27:1*; 51:9+;
Rev.12:3-7; 13:2-11; 16:13; 20:2
See also under 'Serpent(s)'.
[*NIV translates as 'serpent';
+NIV translates as 'monster']

Drink Often used METAPHORICALLY for the receiving of either the blessings or punishments from God. (See the context for explanation in each case).
Job.6:4; 21:20; Ps.36:8; 60:3(AV only); Ps.75:8; 80:5; Pro.9:5; Isa.51:22; Jer.8:14; 9:15; 23:15; 25:15-28; Ezek.23:32; Obad.16; Hab.2:16; Matt.20:22; Mk.10:38,39; Jn.4:14; 6:54,56; 7:37; 18:11; 1 Cor.10:4,21; 11:25,29; 12:13; Rev.14:8,10

Dry Grass See under 'Chaff'.

Dust

i. A METAPHOR for the physical body of man without the soul. Hence also used metaphorically for death (i.e. physical death).
Gen.3:19; 18:27; Job 7:21; 10:9; 17:16; 20:11; 21:26; 34:15; Ps.22:15,29; 30:9; 103:14; 104:29; Ecc.3:20; 12:7; Isa.26:19; Dan.12:2

ii. A SIMILE for a vast number or a amount.
Gen.13:16; 28:14; Num.23:10; 1 Ki.20:10; 2 Chr.1:9; Job 22:24; 27:16; Ps.78:27; Zech.9:3

iii. A METAPHOR for sorrow and humiliation. Either a godly

sorrow with repentance or the
bitter sorrow of the unrepentant -
the context must guide in each
case.
Josh.7:6; 1 Sam.2:8; 1 Ki.16:2;
Job 2:12; 16:15; 40:13; 42:6;
Ps.7:5; 44:25; 72:9; 119:25;
Isa.2:10*; 29:4; 47:1; 49:23;
52:2; Lam.2:10; 3:29;
Ezek.27:30; Mic.1:10; 7:17;
Nah.3:18(AV only);
Rev.18:19
[*NIV translates as 'ground']

iv.   A METAPHOR for insignificance
        or nothingness.
        2 Ki.13:7; 2 Chr.34:4(AV only);
        Job 5:6*; Isa.26:5; 29:5; 40:15
        [*NIV translates as 'soil']

Dwelling place   See under 'Tent'.

Eagle   i.   A METONYMY for swiftness or
                    speed. Often used to describe the
                    rapid progress of invading armies,
                    or the swiftness of God's angelic
                    messengers.
                    Deut.28:49; Job 9:26; Pro.23:5;
                    Jer.48:40; Ezek.1:10; 10:14;
                    17:3,7; Dan.7:4; Hos.8:1;
                    Hab.1:8*;
                    Rev.4:7; 12:14, etc.
                    [*NIV translates as 'vulture']

        ii.   A SIMILE for the wonderful
               protection and care that God has
               for his people.
               Ex.19:4; Deut.32:11

        iii.   A SIMILE for pride and false
               security.
               Jer.49:16; Obad.4

iv. A SIMILE for the restoration of youthfulness and vigour.
Ps.103:5; Isa.40:31

v. A SYMBOL for the appropriate arrival of the time of judgment.
Matt.24:28*; Luke 17:37*
[*NIV translates as 'vultures']

Ear

A METONYMY for attentive hearing.
AV only - Job 36:10; Ps.77:1; Hos.5:1
AV and NIV - 2 Ki.19:16; Neh.1:6;
Ps.31:2; Pro.18:15; Isa.50:5;
Mk.8:18; Rev.2:7, etc.

Earth, Earthly,
Way of the earth

i. A METAPHOR for the earth's population of human beings.
See also under 'World'.
Gen.11:9; 1 Chr.16:33; Ps.48:2;
96:13; Isa.11:4; 45:22;
Jer.4:28; Hab.2:14;
Lk.12:51; 18:8; Rev.13:12;
19:2, etc.

ii. A METAPHOR for earthly-carnally-materialistically-minded people.
Ps.10:18;
Jn.3:31; 1 Cor.15:47; Phil.3:19;
James 3:15; Rev.13:11

iii. A METAPHOR for mortal people as they are subject to death and decay.
Josh.23:14; 1 Ki.2:2;
2 Cor.4:7*; 5:1
[*NIV translates as 'jars of clay']

iv. A METAPHOR for the place where living people are found as

opposed (or in contrast) to the
grave and death.
Ex.9:15; Josh.7:9; 2 Sam.4:11;
Job 18:17; Ps.34:16; 109:15;
Pro.2:22*; 30:14; Jer.10:11;
Nah.2:13;
Acts 22:22
[*NIV translates as 'land']

Earthquake   A METAPHOR for a sudden and violent
change in society (e.g. governments
collapsing). These are seen as
expressions of God's wrath.
Rev.6:12; 8:5; 11:13,19; 16:18;
(see also Hag.2:6,7; Heb.12:26,27)

Eat(ing)   i.   A METAPHOR for having close
fellowship with someone. Often
used for the fellowship of
believers with the Lord. (A meal
was an expression of fellowship in
Bible lands.)
Gen.18:8; 19:3; Ex.12:8; 29:32;
Lev.6:16; 8:31; Num.18:11;
Deut.12:15; 2 Chr.30:18;
Isa.55:1,2;
Matt.26:26; Mk.14:22; Jn.6:53;
Acts 11:3; 1 Cor.10:3,18;
11:20-24; Rev.2:7, etc.

             ii.   A METAPHOR for being
completely destroyed.
Lev.26:38*; Num.24:8*;
Deut.28:33; Ps.27:2*; Ecc.5:11+;
Isa.51:8; Mic.3:3; Nah.3:15*
[*NIV translates as 'devour';
+NIV translates as 'consume']

             iii. A METAPHOR for experiencing
the rewards or results of one's

works or efforts, whether they be good or bad: the context must decide which is meant.
Pro.1:31; 18:21; Isa.3:10 [AV only]

iv.   A METAPHOR for reading and understanding God's Word.
Jer.15:16; Ezek.3:1;
Rev.10:9,10

See under 'Meat' and 'Taste'.

Egypt   A TYPE of our corrupt world with its wealth, human wisdom, idolatry and its persecution of God's people.
Rev.11:8

Enlightened   See under 'Shine(s)'.

Eye(s)   i.   A METAPHOR for God's watchful care and guardianship of his people.
Deut.32:10; 1 Ki.8:29,52;
2 Chr.6:20,40; Ezra 5:5;
Job 36:7; Ps.32:8(AV only);
33:18; 34:15; Jer.24:6;
Amos 9:8; Zech.12:4;
1 Pet.3:12

ii.   A METAPHOR for the omniscience of God or the watchfulness of heavenly creatures. Sometimes coupled with his judgments on the wicked.
2 Sam.22:28; 2 Chr.16:9;
Job 34:21; Ps.11:4; 139:16;
Jer.16:17; Ezek.1:18; 10:12;
Amos 9:4; Zech.3:9; 4:10;
Heb.4:13; Rev.1:14; 2:18;
4:6,8; 5:6; 19:12

iii.   A METAPHOR for one's desires
        or intentions or hopes, whether
        they be good or bad.
        Gen.39:7[AVonly]; Deut.15:9
        [AV only]; Job 31:7; 41:18;
        Ps.101:3; 119:37; 131:1; 141:8;
        Pro.17:24; 23:6[AV only];
        Ecc.1:8; 2:10; Isa.3:16;
        Lam.2:4; Ezek.20:7,8; Zech.9:1;
        Matt.6:22; Mk.7:22[AV only];
        Lk.11:34; 2 Pet.2:14; 1 Jn.2:16,
        etc.

iv.   A   METAPHOR   for
        understanding. Often referring to
        spiritual understanding.
        Gen.3:7; Num.22:31; Job 28:21;
        Ps.19:8; 36:1; 119:18; Ecc.2:14;
        Isa.6:10; 42:7; Dan.7:8;
        Matt.13:15; Acts 26:18;
        Rom.11:8,10; Gal.3:1; Eph.1:18;
        1 Jn.2:11[AV only]; Rev.3:18, etc.

v.   A METAPHOR for one's
        estimation or judgment of oneself
        or another person or thing.
        AV only - Gen.16:4,5; Ex.5:21;
        Deut.24:1; Jud.17:6;
        2 Sam.19:27; 1 Chr.21:23;
        Esth.8:5; Ps.15:4; Pro.17:8;
        21:2; Zech.8:6
        AV and NIV - Gen.3:6;
        Num.20:12*; 1 Sam.20:3;
        1 Ki.11:33; 2 Ki.10:30;
        Job 32:1; Isa.5:21
        [*NIV translates as 'sight']

vi.   A METAPHOR for one being
        without pity or mercy.,
        AV only - Deut.7:16; 13:8;

19:21; 25:12; Isa.13:18;
Ezek.5:11; 7:4,9; 8:18; 9:5; 16:5
AV and NIV - Micah 4:11

vii. A METAPHOR for grief or
sorrow.
Ps.88:9; Jer.9:1,18; 13:17;
14:17; Lam.1:16; 2:11,18;
3:48,49;
Rev.7:17; 21:4

Face i. A METAPHOR for being in the
presence of or being in the sight of
someone. Often used of God.
AV only - Gen.16:8; Ex.2:15;
Lev.19:32; Num.19:3; 2 Ki.18:24;
2 Chr.6:42; Ps.5:8; Jer.32:31;
Hos.7:2;
Matt.11:10; Mk.1:2; Lk.2:31;
Acts 2:25; Rev.12:14; 20:11;
AV and NIV - Ex.33:11;
Deut.7:10; Job 1:11; Ps.27:8;
67:1; 105:4;
1 Cor.13:12; Gal.2:11;
Rev.22:4, etc.

ii. A METAPHOR for one's aims or
goals or for one's attitude. May be
either good or bad, according to
the context.
AV only - Gen.31:21;
2 Chr.35:22; Pro.21:29; Dan.9:3;
Lk.9:51;
AV and NIV - Lev.17:10; 20:6;
Num.24:1; Pro.7:13; Ecc.8:1;
Jer.2:27; 32:33; Ezek.14:4

iii. A METAPHOR for God's favour.
Num.6:25; Ps.17:15; 31:16;
67:1; 80:3,7,19; 119:135;

Jer.18:17; 32:31*
[*NIV translates as 'sight']

iv.   A METAPHOR for someone's
        feelings or emotions (as shown by
        one's face).
        AV only - 2 Chr.32:21; Jer.7:19;
        Ezek.3:8;
        AV and NIV - Ex.3:6;
        2 Sam.2:22; Job 11:15; Ps.69:7

v.   A SIMILE representing the
        person's character to whom the
        face belongs.
        Ezek.1:10; 10:14; 41:18,19;
        Dan.10:6; 2 Cor.4:6; James 1:23;
        Rev.4:7; 9:7; 10:1

Fan   See under 'Winnow'.

Fat, Fatness   i.   A METAPHOR for the best part of
                        something or for the abundance of
                        good things or for prosperity.
                        AV only - Gen.49:20; Num.13:20;
                        1 Chr.4:40; Neh.9:25; Pro.11:25;
                        Isa.5:17; Ezek.34:14; Hab.1:16,
                        etc.

                  ii.   A METAPHOR for dullness or
                        insensitivity. Maybe as a direct
                        result of material prosperity.
                        AV only - Deut.31:20;
                        AV and NIV - Deut.32:15;
                        Isa.6:10*; Jer.5:18; Ezek.34:20
                        [*NIV translates as 'calloused']

Field   See under 'Grass'.

Fig Tree   i.   A SYMBOL for the nation of
                        Israel. They appeared to be

religious but this was only a show because they bore no fruit in their lives.
Matt.21:19-21; Mk.11:13,20,21; Lk.13:6,7; 21:29

ii.   A SYMBOL for the good life. To live under one's fig tree represented a life of peace, joy and prosperity.
1 Ki.4:25; 2 Ki.18:31; Isa.36:16; Mic.4:4; Zech.3:10

Finger of God

A METAPHOR for a display of God working in power in the world in a miraculous way.
Ex.8:19; 31:18; Deut.9:10; Lk.11:20

Fire

i.   A SYMBOL for God's holiness and his great wrath against all sin. This is finally shown in hell.
See also under 'Flame/Flaming' 'Oven'.
Ex.3:2; Lev.9:24; Num.9:16; Deut.1:33; 1 Ki.18:24; 2 Ki.1:10; Ps.78:21; Isa.66:15; Jer.21:12; Lam.2:4; Ezek.1:4; Dan.7:9-11; Amos 1:4; 2:2; Mic.1:4; Nah.1:6; Zech.2:5; Mal.3:2; Matt.3:10; Lk.3:9; Jn.15:6; 1 Cor.3:13; 2 Thess.1:8 (7, NIV); Heb.12:29; Rev.1:14; 8:5; 16:8; 20.9,14,15, etc.

ii.   A SYMBOL for the righteous anger of God's servants and for their God-given power.
Ps.39:3; Jer.5:14; 20:9; Obad.18; Heb.1:7; Rev.11:5

iii.   A METAPHOR for the ravaging (or wasting) effects of sin in a person's life.
Pro.6:27; 16:27; 26:20,21;
Isa.9:18; Hos.7:4,6; Amos 4:11;
Zech.2:5;
James 3:5,6; 5:3; Jude 23;
Rev.9:17,18

iv.   A METAPHOR for a severe trial or testing which has a purifying effect, through the grace of God.
See under 'Furnace'.
Isa.43:2; Zech.13:9;
1 Pet.1:7; Rev.3:18

v.   A SYMBOL for the Holy Spirit, with his empowering, purifying role especially in mind.
Matt.3:11; Lk.3:16; Acts 2:3

vi.   A SYMBOL for the convicting power of the Word of God.
Jer.23:29
Lk.12:49

See also under 'Pillar of fire'.

Firstfruits

A METAPHOR for a deposit guaranteeing that which is to follow and indicating the nature of that fullness. (In the Old Testament, the term is used to speak of 'firstfruit' offerings of grain, wine, cattle and so on, appointed by Moses (Lev.23:10). Such firstfruits were representative of the total harvest, flock, etc. - a thankful indicator that the whole had been given to God.)
Rom.8:23; 11:16; 16:5[AV only];
1 Cor.15:20,23; 16:15; James 1:18;
Rev.14:4

Fist		See under 'Hand'.
Flame, Flaming	i.	A SYMBOL for God's holiness and his righteous indignation against sin. See also under 'Fire' (i). Gen.3:24; Ex.3:2; Judg.13:20; Ps.83:14; 106:18; Isa.5:14; 10:17; 29:6; 66:15; Ezek.20:47; Dan.7:9; Obad.18; Lk.16:24; Heb.1:7; Rev.1:14*; 2:18*; 19:12* [*NIV translates as 'blazing fire']
	ii.	A METAPHOR for the damaging effects of Satan's attacks. See also under 'Fire' (iii). Eph.6:16
Flesh	i.	A METAPHOR for physical human life or of relationship or of family descent. Often used with reference to Christ's human nature. AV only - Acts 2:30; Rom.1:3; 9:3,5; 2 Cor.4:11; Col.1:22; 1 Tim.3:16; 1 Pet.3:18; 1 Jn.4:3; AV and NIV - Jn.1:14; 1 Cor.15:39; Eph.2:15; Heb.2:14; 1 Jn.4:2
	ii.	A METAPHOR for human strength and wisdom. AV only - Jn.8:15; 1 Cor.1:29; Gal.1:16; 3:3; AV and NIV - 1 Chr.32:8; Jer.17:5; Jn.6:63; Eph.6:12; Phil.3:3, etc.

iii.   A METAPHOR for corrupt and
        sinful human nature. Lacking
        spiritual sense and desires, people
        can rise no higher than to seek to
        gratify their bodily appetites or
        be controlled by a defective
        understanding of God and the
        world.
        See also under 'World'.
        AV only - Gcn.6:3,12;
        Rom.3:20; 7:25; 8:1-13; 13:14;
        2 Cor.10:2; Gal.2:16; 5:13,17,24;
        Gal.6:8; Eph.2:3; Col.2:11;
        1 Pet.3:21; 2 Pet.2:10; 1 Jn.2:16;
        Jude 7,8;
        AV and NIV - Jude 23 etc.

iv.   A METAPHOR for something
        being alive and sensitive to God
        (i.e. the opposite of iii.)
        Ezek.11:19; 36:26

v.   To become 'one flesh' is a
        METAPHOR for a very close and
        intimate relationship between two
        persons. It is as though they
        become one. Used to describe
        marriage and the relationship
        between God and his people.
        Gen.2:24;
        Matt.19:5,6 [AV only]; Mk.10:8;
        1 Cor.6:16; Eph.5:29,30;
        Eph.5:31 [NIV only]

Flock   See under 'Sheep'.

Flood   A METAPHOR or SIMILE for
               overwhelming sorrows, temptations or
               dangers.
               AV only - Ps.90:5; Jer.46:7,8;

Dan.11:22;
AV and NIV - Ps.69:15; Isa.28:2*;
59:19; Dan.9:26; Jonah 2:3+; Nah.1:8;
Matt.7:25,27**; Lk.6:48;
Rev.12:15,16++
[*NIV translates as 'flooding down-
pour';
+NIV translates as 'currents';
**NIV translates as 'streams arose';
++NIV translates as 'river' and
'torrents']

Floods   See under 'Streams'.

Flower   See under 'Grass'.

Food   See under 'Meat'.

Forest   A SIMILE for the people of a strong
                    nation.
                    Isa.9:18; 10:18,19,34; 29:17;
                    32:15,19; Jer.21:14; 46:23;
                    Ezek.20:46,47; Zech.11:2

Former Rain   See under 'Water(s)'.

Fornication   A METAPHOR for spiritual
                    unfaithfulness. The worship of idols or
                    money, etc. rather than devotion to God.
                    See also under 'Adultery' and 'Harlot'.
                    2 Chr.21:11*; Isa.23:17*; Ezek.16:29+;
                    Rev.14:8**; 17:2,4**; 18:3**; 19:2**
                    [*NIV translates as 'prostitute';
                    +NIV translates as 'promiscuity';
                    **NIV translates as 'adulteries']

Foundation   A SYMBOL or a METAPHOR for
                    Christ and for his teaching. We must be
                    truly joined to Christ and upheld by him
                    if we want to be truly and eternally safe.
                    Ps.11:3; Pro.10:25 [AV only]; Isa.28:16;

Zech.4:9;
Lk.6:48,49; 1 Cor.3:10-12;
Eph.2:20; Rev.21:14,19

Foundation of the
world

A METAPHOR for the creation of the
world and for the beginning of time.
AV only - Matt.13:35; 25:34;
Lk.11:50; Jn.17:24; Eph.1:4;
Heb.4:3; 9:26; 1 Pet.1:20;
Rev.13:8; 17:8
AV and NIV - Isa.40:21*;
[*NIV translates as 'founded']

Four

The number which SYMBOLIZES
creation: e.g. the four living creatures
represent God's angelic messengers to
the whole world (Rev.4:6): i.e. to all four
points of the compass.
Gen.2:10; Ezek.1:5-17; 10:9-21;
37:9; Dan.7:2,3,17; 11:4;
Zech.1:18,20; 6:1;
Matt.24:31; Mk.13:27; Rev.4:6,8;
5:14; 6:6; 7:1; 9:13[AV only],14;
14:3; 15:7; 19:4

Foursquare

The shape that is used to SYMBOLIZE
perfect holiness.
Ex.27:1*; 28:16*; Ezek.40:47*; 48:20*;
Rev.21:16*, etc.
[*NIV translates as 'square']

Fox(es)

A METAPHOR for people who are
cunning, treacherous and vicious.
Song.2:15; Ezek.13:4*; Lk.13:32
[*NIV translates as 'jackals']

Frankincense

See under 'Incense'.

Fruit(s),
Fruitful(ness)

i.   A METAPHOR for one's character and its effects in the life. In a

believer the Holy Spirit produces a good character and deeds. In an unbeliever sin produces a bad character and evil works.
AV only - Pro.12:12; Jer.32:19; Mic.7:13;
Rom.6:21; Phil.4:17;
AV and NIV - Gen.49:22; Ps.1:3; 92:14; Pro.11:30; Song.4:13,16; Isa.3:10; 27:6; Jer.6:19;
Hos.10:1; Amos 2:9;
Matt.3:10; 7:17; 12:33; 13:23*; 21:19; Mk.4:20*; 12:2; Lk.8:8*; 13:6; 20:10; Jn.15:2-8;
Rom.7:4; Gal.5:22; Eph.5:9;
Col.1:10; Heb.13:15;
James 3:18+; Jude 12, etc.
[*NIV translates as 'crop';
+NIV translates as 'harvest']

ii.   A METAPHOR for those who have been won by the gospel and converted to Christianity.
Jn.4:36*; 12:24+; Rom.1:13*; Phil.1:22; Col.1:6
[*NIV translates as 'harvest(s);
+NIV translates as 'many seeds']

iii. A METAPHOR for the blessings we receive from God through the gospel.
Ezek.36:11; 47:12; Hos.14:8;
Amos 6:12;
Rev.22:2

iv.   The fruit of the body, or of the womb, is often used as a METAPHOR for children.
AV only - Ex.21:22; Ps.127:3; 132:11; Isa.13:18;

Lk.1:42; Acts 2:30, etc.
AV and NIV - Gen.1:22; Ex.1:7;
Deut.28:4,11; Ps.128:3;
Ezek.17:9; 19:12; Mic.6:7

Furnace   i.   A METAPHOR for the place of
                               severe testings and trials. By this
                               means believers are purified and
                               strengthened in their faith through
                               the grace of God.
                               See also under 'Fire'.
                               Deut.4:20; 1 Ki.8:51; Pro.17:3;
                               Pro.27:21; Isa.48:10

                       ii.   A SYMBOL for the holiness and
                               purity of God or of his Word, the
                               Bible.
                               Gen.15:17*; Ex.19:18; Ps.12:6;
                               Isa.31:9;
                               Rev.1:15
                               [*NIV translates as 'blazing
                               torch']

                       iii.   A METAPHOR for the place of
                               the punishment of the wicked.
                               That is hell, where God's wrath
                               rages without ceasing.
                               Ezek.22:18-22;
                               Matt.13:42,50; Rev.9:2

                               See also under 'Oven'.

Gall   i.   A METAPHOR for severe trials
                               or afflictions.
                               Ps.69:21; Jer.8:14*; 9:15*;
                               23:15*; Lam.3:5+,19
                               [*NIV translates as 'poisoned
                               water';
                               +NIV translates as 'bitterness']

| | ii. | A METAPHOR for the bitter and unpleasant effects of sin.
Deut.29:18*; 32:32+;
Job 20:14**; Amos 6:12*;
Acts 8:23+
[*NIV translates as 'poison';
+NIV translates as 'bitterness';
**NIV translates as 'venom'] |

Garden

A SIMILE describing the life of a person or of a people, as it is cultivated, beautiful and fruitful.
See also under 'Fruit'.
Num.24:6; Job 8:16; Song.4:12-16; 5:1; 6:2,11*; Isa.51:3; 58:11; 61:11; Jer.31:12; Ezek.36:35
[*NIV translates as 'grove']

Garment

i.   A SYMBOL representing a person's character or condition or behaviour, e.g. the wedding garment in Matt.22:11 (NIV translates as 'wedding clothes') represents the imputed righteousness of Christ which puts sinners into a condition where they are acceptable to God.
AV only - Ps.69:11;
AV and NIV - Ps.73:6*; 104:2;
Ps.109:18,19+; Ecc.9:8*;
Isa.52:1; 59:6*,17; 61:3,10;
63:1; Dan.7:9*; Zech.3:3*-4;
Mal.2:16;
Matt.22:11,12*; Jude 23*;
Rev.1:13**; 3:4; 16:15
[*NIV translates variously, 'clothes', 'clothing', etc.;
+NIV translates as 'cloak';
**NIV translates as 'robe']

ii.   A SIMILE for something that is prone to corruption and decay, in the same way as a garment can become moth-eaten and worn out.
Job 13:28; Ps.102:26; Isa.50:9; 51:6,8;
Matt.9:16; Mk.2:21; Lk.5:36; James 5:2*
[*NIV translates as 'clothes']

Gate(s)   i.   A METAPHOR for the means of entry into a place or into the presence of a person or a number of persons, e.g. into heaven, into the presence of God and the holy angels. See also under 'Door'.
Gen.28:17; Ps.9:13,14; 24:7,9; 87:2; 100:4; 118:19,20; Pro.8:3; 31:31; Isa.26:2; 38:10; 54:12; 62:10; Jer.7:2; Obad.13;
Matt.7:13,14; Lk.13:24*;
Heb.13:12; Rev.21:12,13,21,25, etc.
[*NIV translates as 'door']

ii.   A METAPHOR for the place of power and authority. In Old Testament times, authoritative decisions were made by the Jewish elders in the large area connected with the main gates of a city. The place where issues are discussed and decisions are made, e.g. 'the gates of hell' means the power and the schemes of Satan and the fallen angels.
AV only - Gen.22:17; Job 5:4; 31:21; Pro.22:22; Isa.29:21; Jer.14:2; Amos 5:10; Zech.8:16;
AV and NIV - Gen.24:60;
Ps.107:16; 127:5; Pro.14:19;

24:7; 31:23; Isa.3:26; 13:2;
14:31; Lam.2:9; Ezek.21:15;
Mic.1:9,12; 2:13;
Matt.16:18, etc.

Give light	See under 'Shine(s).

Glass   i.   A METAPHOR for the holiness and peacefulness of heaven.
Rev.4:6; 15:2; 21:18,21

                ii.   Used in the sense of a reflecting mirror. This is a SYMBOL used to describe the way in which believers see spiritual and eternal truths. Either the truth about Christ and his work or the truth about themselves as God sees them.
1 Cor.13:12*; 2 Cor.3:18+;
James 1:23**
[*NIV translates as 'poor reflection';
+NIV translates as 'reflect';
**NIV translates as 'mirror']

Go   See under 'Walk(s)'.

Glean, Gleaning(s)   i.   A SYMBOL representing those faithful believers who remain after a period of trial and persecution.
Isa.17:6; 24:13

                ii.   A METAPHOR used to describe the very thorough nature of God's judgments.
Jer.6:9; 49:9[AV only]; see also Mic.7:1.

Goat(s)   i.   The goats used for the sin offering and the scapegoat were TYPES of

Christ. They show that Christ had to become a curse for us as he suffered and died in our place.
Lev.16:8,10,26; 23:19;
Num.7:16; 15:24; 2 Chr.29:21;
Heb.9:12,13,etc.

ii.   A SYMBOL for the forces of Alexander the Great. The goat was an emblem of the country of Macedonia.
Dan.8:5,8,21

iii.   A METAPHOR for the wicked and impenitent who will be condemned to eternal punishment for their sins.
Zech.10:3[AV only];
Matt.25:32,33

Gold(en)   i.   A SYMBOL used to represent the very precious and lasting nature of spiritual things such as faith or the Scriptures.
Ex.25:11; 28:15; Job 23:10;
28:16; Ps.19:20; 119:72;
Pro.16:16; 25:11; Isa.60:17;
Zech.4:2;
1 Cor.3:12; 2 Tim.2:20;
1 Pet.1:7; Rev.1:12,13; 2:1;
3:18; 5:8; 8:3; 14:14; 15:7;
21:18,21, etc.

ii.   A SYMBOL for the empty attractions and glamour of the things of this world. These are the things that lure unbelievers into lusting after and worshipping them.
Pro.11:22; Jer.4:30; Lam.4:1;

Dan.2:38;
James 5:3; Rev.9:7,20; 17:4;
18:12,16, etc.

Grape(s)   i.   A SYMBOL sometimes used to represent hopeful signs of faith and obedience to God.
Hos.9:10;
Matt.7:16; Lk.6:44

ii.   A sour grape is used as a METAPHOR for some grievous sin and its bitter effects.
Deut.32:32; Isa.5;4; Jer.31:29; Ezek.18:2

iii.   The harvesting of grapes is used as a SYMBOL to represent a terrible judgment.
See also under 'Harvest'.
Job 15:33; Isa.18:5; Jer.8:13; 25:30;
Rev.14:18,19

Grasp   See under 'Hand'.

Grass   i.   A SIMILE for a large number or for a great abundance of something.
Job 5:25; Ps.72:16; Isa.44:4

ii.   A SIMILE for mortal people. Like the grass they wither and die. But in life they are also wonderfully cared for by God.
Ps.37:2; 90:5; 92:7; 102:4,11; 103:15; 129:6; Isa.40:6-8; 51:12;
Matt.6:30; Lk.12:28;
James 1:10*,11+; 1 Pet.1:24
[*NIV translates as 'wild flower'; +NIV translates as 'plant']

iii.   Grass upon which rain or dew descends is used as a SYMBOL to represent reviving blessings from the Lord.
Ps.72:6*; Pro.19:12; Mic.5:7
[*NIV translates as 'mown field']

Grasshopper(s)   A SIMILE for people who are relatively small and weak.
Num.13:33; Isa.40:22

Ground   See under 'Dust'.

Grove   See under 'Garden'.

Hail, Hailstones, Hailstorm   A SYMBOL used to represent God's judgments on his enemies.
Ex.9:18*-33; 10:5-15; Josh.10:11;
Ps.18:12,13[AV only]; 78:47,48;
105:32; Isa.28:2*,17; 30:30;
Ezek.13:11,13; 38:22;
Rev.8:7; 11:19*; 16:21
[*NIV translates as 'hailstorm']

Hair(s)

i.   A SYMBOL for one's being dedicated to God by not cutting one's hair. In case of defilement the hair had to be completely shorn.
Num.6:5-21

ii.   Sometimes used as a SYMBOL for the least important part of one's body, e.g. 'not a hair from your head shall perish' means you will not suffer any harm whatsoever.
1 Sam.14:45; Dan.3:27;
Matt.10:30; Lk.12:7; 21:18;
Acts 27:34

Hall   See under 'House'.

Hand(s)

i.   A METAPHOR for authority or power or vigour, e.g. 'years of right hand' means early manhood when one is at the peak of one's strength. The right hand of God signifies the sovereignty of the Almighty.
Ex.6:1; Judg.1:35[AV only];
2 Sam.24:14; 2 Ki.13:5[AV only];
Ezra 7:9; Job 15:25*; Ps.31:8;
Pro.12:14; Isa.11:11; Jer.12:7;
Lam.1:14; Ezek.28:9; Dan.4:35;
Joel 3:8[AV only];
Mic.2:1[AV only]; Hab.3:4;
Mk.14:41; Lk.1:66; Jn.10:39+;
Acts 11:21; Rom.8:34; Eph.1:20;
Col.3:1; Heb.1:3; 1 Pet.3:22;
Rev.1:16,20; 2:1, etc.
[*NIV translates as 'fist';
+NIV translates as 'grasp']

ii.   A SYNECDOCHE for instrumentality. The means or the person by which something is done, or by which a message is delivered, etc.
AV only - Ex.4:13; Josh.20:9;
1 Ki.2:25; 2 Ki.14:25;
2 Chr.10:15; Ezra 1:8;
Neh.11:24; Job 27:11;
Acts 7:25; Rev.19:2;
AV and NIV - Deut.13:9;
1 Sam.18:25; 2 Sam.3:18;
Pro.10:4; Isa.10:5; Jer.18:4;
Ezek.8:3; Dan.5:5; Zech.4:10;
Lk.22:21; Col.4:18; Rev.8:4, etc.

iii.   A METAPHOR for being in one's
       possession or under one's control,
       care or protection.
       Gen.9:2; Ex.33:22;
       Lev.25:28[AV only]; 1 Sam.21:3;
       Ezra 7:14; Job 12:10;
       Ps.95:7[AV only]; Pro.6:3;
       Ecc.9:1; Isa.49:2; Dan.5:23;
       Jn.10:28; Rev.5:1,7; 13:16, etc.

iv.   A METAPHOR for an assault or a
       chastening, e.g. 'The hand of the
       Lord was against them to destroy
       them' (Deut.2:15).
       Ex.3:20; Deut.2:15; Judg.2:15;
       Ruth 1:13; 1 Sam.5:6,7;
       2 Sam.18:12; Job 13:21; Ps.75:8;
       106:26; Isa.50:11; Lam.2:8;
       Amos 9:2; Zech.14:13;
       Matt.3:12; Lk.3:17; Acts 13:11,
       etc.

v.   A METAPHOR for either the
       giving or the receiving of
       something.
       Gen.33:10[AV only]; Job 2:10[AV
       only]; Job 35:7; Ps.16:11;
       Pro.3:16; 31:20; Ecc.2:24

vi.   A METAPHOR for being
       submissive to or dependent on
       someone.
       Ps.123:2; Lam.5:6[AV only];
       1 Pet.5:6; Rev.13:16; 14:9

vii.   'At hand' is often used as a
       METAPHOR for proximity or
       nearness either in place or in time.
       AV only - Deut.15:9; 1 Sam.9:8;
       Isa.13:6; Jer.23:23; Ezek.12:23;

Joel 1:15;
Matt.4:17; Mk.1:15; Lk.21:30;
Jn.2:13; Rom.13:12; Phil.4:5;
1 Pet.4:7; Rev.1:3; 22:10 etc.
AV and NIV - Ps.16:8

viii.   Hands lifted up or stretched out
SYMBOLIZES an attitude of
worship, praise or prayer.
1 Ki.8:22; 2 Chr.6:12,13,29;
Job 17:3[AV only]; Ps.28:2;
44:20; 63:4; 88:9; 119:48;
134:2; 141:2; 143:6; Pro.17:18;
22:26; Lam.2:19;
Acts 17:25; 1 Tim.2:8

ix.   The laying on of hands
SYMBOLIZES the giving of
some blessing or spiritual gift, or
may be used to SYMBOLIZE
setting apart of a person to some
special office or work.
Deut.34:9;
Matt.19:13; Mk.10:16; Acts 8:18;
1 Tim.4:14; 2 Tim.1:6; Heb.6:2,
etc.

x.   A METAPHOR for being in
agreement with someone to help
or support each other.
1 Sam.22:17 [AV only];2 Sam.14:19;
Job 17:3[AV only]; Pro.17:18;
22:26; Hos.7:5

xi.   The raising of one's hand is often
used as a SYMBOL for one's
pledge of faithfulness in making a
promise or in taking a vow.
Deut.32:40; Isa.62:8; Ezek.17:18

xii.   A METAPHOR for a person's
        actions or deeds, whether good or
        bad, as seen by its context, e.g.
        'clean hands' means one's
        behaviour has been free from
        guilt.
        Gen.4:11; 20:5; 1 Sam.24:10;
        1 Chr.12:17; Job 11:14; 16:17;
        17:9; Ps.7:3; 18:34; 26:10;
        58:2; 125:3; 144:1; Pro.6:17;
        Ecc.7:26; Isa.1:15; 33:15;
        59:3,6; Ezek.23:37; Jon.3:8[AV
        only]; Mic.5:12[AV only];
        James 4:8

xiii.   The stretching out of hands when
        used of God SYMBOLIZES his
        gracious invitation to sinners to
        repent. When used of people it
        can represent an attitude of grief
        and despair and the seeking of
        comfort and relief.
        Pro.1:24; Isa.65:2; Jer.4:31;
        Lam.1:17;
        Rom.10:21

xiv.   The taking of one's life in one's
        hands is a METAPHOR for
        risking one's life.
        Judg.12:3; 1 Sam.28:21;
        Job 13:14; Psa.119:109

xv.   The clapping of hands can
        SYMBOLIZE:
        a. rejoicing
           2 Ki.11:12; Ps.47:1
           Nah.3:19
or   b. self-praise
           Job 34:37

or   c. the giving of a command or summons
Ezek.21:14,17

xvi.   The phrase 'at one's hand' is a METAPHOR for one's responsibility or accountability.
AV only - Ezek.3:18,20; 33:6;

xvii.   The right and left hands are used figuratively in several different ways:
a. meaning both sides
Ex.14:22

or   b. consistent faithfulness
2 Ki.22:2[AV only]

or   c. the inability to distinguish left and right hands is a METAPHOR for those who are below the age of discernment, i.e. children.
Jon.4:11

or   d. Not letting one's left hand know what one's right hand is doing is a METAPHOR for doing something without self-consciousness.
Matt.6:3

or   e. When Christ places the sheep on his right hand and goats on his left, this means he will separate his elect from all others on the day of judgment.
Matt.25:33

Harlot(s)   A METAPHOR for those who are unfaithful to God.
See also under 'Adultery/Fornication'.
Isa.1:21; Jer.2:20*; 3:1*-8+;

Ezek.16:15-41*; 23:5-44*; Hos.2:5**;
3:3*; 4:15+; Mic.1:7*; Nah.3:4;
Rev.17:5*
[*NIV translates as 'prostitute';
+NIV translates as 'adultery';
**NIV translates as 'unfaithful']

Harvest   i.   A METAPHOR for the gathering
                         of people to face a terrible judg-
                         ment.
                         See also under 'Grapes'.
                         Jer.51:33; Hos.6:11; Joel 3:13;
                         Matt.13:30,39; Rev.14:15

                 ii.   A METAPHOR for the gathering
                         of believers to Christ in response
                         to the gospel.
                         See also under 'Sheaves' and
                         'Fruit'.
                         Matt.9:37,38; Lk.10:2; Jn.4:35

Head(s)   i.   A METAPHOR for one who rules,
                         e.g. the crushing of the serpent's
                         head in Gen.3:15 represents
                         Christ's breaking Satan's rule
                         over fallen mankind.
                         Gen.3:15; Num.17:3; Deut.28:13;
                         Judg.10:18; 2 Sam.22:44;
                         1 Chr.29:11; Ps.18:43; Isa.7:8,9;
                         Hos.1:11 [AV only];
                         1 Cor.11:3*; Eph.1:22; 4:15*;
                         5:23; Col.1:18*; 2:10,19*;
                         Rev.13:1,3; 17:9, etc.
                         (*Some modern commentators
                         have suggested that 'head' is used
                         in some places in the New
                         Testament as a METAPHOR for
                         source or origin, rather than
                         authority.)

ii.   A SYNECDOCHE for the whole person, e.g. to place something on a person's head may be used to SYMBOLIZE their receiving a blessing or responsibility, guilt or punishment, as the context indicates.
Gen.49:26; Ex.29:10; Lev.8:14; Deut.33:16; Josh.2:19;
1 Sam.25:39; 2 Sam.1:16;
2 Chr.6:23; Neh.4:4; Esth.9:25; Ps.7:16; 23:5; 68:21; Pro.10:6; 25:22; Ezek.11:21; 22:31;
Acts 18:6, etc.

iii.   To lift up one's head is sometimes used as a METAPHOR for their deliverance or exaltation even if it was very temporary as in Gen.40:19 [NIV says 'lift off'].
Gen.40:13,19; 2 Ki.25:27[AV only]; Job 10:15; Ps.3:3; 27:6; 83:2; 110:7

iv.   The uncovering or shaving of one's head, or covering it with ashes, SYMBOLIZED their deep sorrow or mourning.
Lev.10:6[NIV, margin only]; 21:5; Job 1:20; Isa.15:2; Jer.14:3,4; Ezek.7:18; 44:20; Rev.18:19

v.   For something to go over one's head is a METAPHOR for being overwhelmed or oppressed.
Ps.38:4[AV only]; 66:12

vi.   A SYMBOL for one's being dedicated to God by not cutting

one's hair. In case of defilement the hair had to be completely shorn.
Deut.21:12; Judg.13:5

Health   See under 'Wound'.

Heart   A METAPHOR for a person's inner self which includes the understanding, the emotions and the will. Either one or two or all three of them as indicated by the context.
AV only - Job 9:4; Ecc.1:13; Dan.1:8;
Matt.12:35; Mk.7:21; Jn.13:2;
Acts 5:33; 1 Cor.2:9; 1 Pet.3:4;
AV and NIV - Gen.6:5; Ex.4:14;
Deut.11:13; 1 Sam.16:7; 1 Ki.3:9;
Ps.119:36; 139:23; Pro.23:7;
Isa.65:14; Jer.17:10; Ezek.14:4;
Lk.2:19; Rom.6:17; 2 Cor.9:7;
Eph.6:6; Phil.1:7; 1 Tim.1:5;
Heb.4:12; Jas.3:14; 2 Pet.1:19;
1 Jn.3:20; Rev.2:23; 18:7, etc.

Hedge   i.   A METAPHOR for a boundary or limits or for defences.
Job 1:10; 3:23; Ps.80:12*;
89:40*; Isa.5:5; Hos.2:6(AV only)
[*NIV translates as 'wall(s)']

                ii.   A METAPHOR for unfruitfulness and troublesomeness.
Pro.15:19*; Mic.7:4
[*NIV translates as 'blocked']

Heifer   i.   A TYPE of the Lord Jesus Christ, whose blood, applied to a sinner's conscience, cleanses it and

removes the terror of approaching
God.
Gen.15:9; Num.19:2-10;
Deut.21:3-6; 1 Sam.16:2;
Heb.9:13, cf.14

ii.   A SIMILE for sinful people
        who can resemble heifers in
        some ways, e.g. in their
        greediness, stubbornness and in
        their youthful vigorousness.
        Jer.46:20; 50:11; Hos.4:16; 10:11

Helmet, or   A SYMBOL for a strong defence for a
The strength of   vital area. As Ephraim protected the
the head   northern border of Judah, so the
                      assurance of salvation protects the
                      Christian from, for example, confusion
                      about the purpose of life.
                      Ps.60:7; 108:8;
                      Eph.6:17; 1 Thess.5:8

Hid   See under 'Veil(ed)'.

High ones   See under 'Tree(s)'.

High place   See under 'Mount(ain)'.

Hill(s), Hilltop   i   A SYMBOL for a place of
                            authority or for one who rules. It
                            can be used either of God or of
                            people, as the context shows.
                            See also under 'Mount(ain)'.
                            Ps.2:6; 3:4; 15:1; 24:3; Isa.2:2;
                            41:15; Ezek.6:3; 36:4,6; Mic.4:1;
                            Hab.3:6;
                            Rev.17:9

                      ii.   The hills producing rich harvests
                            is used as a SYMBOL to denote

the rich blessings God has in store
for his people.
Gen.49:26; Deut.33:25; Ps.50:10;
65:12; 72:3,16; 147:8; Song.4:6;
Isa.30:25; 49:9; Joel 3:18;
Amos 9:13

iii.   A METAPHOR for the obstacles
produced by sin which need to be
removed in the redemption of
God's people.
See also under 'Mount(ain)'.
Song.2:8,17; Isa.40:4

iv.   The place where the Israelites
worshipped idols. Hills therefore
came to represent unfaithfulness
to God in certain contexts.
See also under 'Mount(ain)'.
Isa.57:7; Jer.2:20; 3:6,23; 13:27;
17:2

v.   Sometimes used as a PERSON-
IFICATION of a part of the earth,
as God's creation.
Ps.114:4,6; Isa.55:12; Mic.6:1;
Nah.1:5; Hab.3:6

vi.   A METAPHOR for a place of
refuge where one may flee from
threats   and   dangers.
Ps.121:1; Jer.49:16; Hos.10:8;
Lk.23:30

Hill country   See under 'Mount(ain)'.

Honey, Honeycomb   i.   A SIMILE for that which actually
is, or which only appears to be,
pleasant and desirable.
Ps.19:10; 119:103; Pro.5:3;

16:24; 24:13; Song.4:11; 5:1;
Ezek.3:3;
Rev.10:9

ii.   A SYNECDOCHE for an
abundance of good things.
Ex.3:8,17; Lev.20:24; Num.13:27;
Deut.6:3; Josh.5:6; Isa.7:22;
Jer.11:5; Ezek.16:13, etc.

Horn(s)   i.   A METAPHOR for strength and
honour. Sometimes used in a bad
sense to denote pride.
Deut.33:17; 1 Sam.2:1;
Sam.22:3; 1 Chr.25:5*;
Job 16:15[AV only]; Ps.18:2;
75:4,5,10; 89:17,24; 112:9;
132:17; 148:14; Jer.48:25;
Lam.2:3,17; Amos 6:13*;
Mic.4:13
[*NIV margin only]

ii.   A METAPHOR either for
authority itself or for the one who
exercises authority, e.g. a king.
Ezek.29:21; Dan.7:8-24; 8:3-20;
Zech.1:18-21:
Rev.5:6; 12:2; 13:1,11; 17:3-16

Horse(s)   i.   A SYMBOL for power and might
of human or demonic origin.
Ps.147:10; Pro.21:31; Isa.2:7;
31:1,3; 43:17; Jer.4:13; 6:23;
Hos.1:7; Hab.1:8;
Rev.9:7; 19:18

ii.   A SYMBOL for the power of
angels and the host of heaven.
2 Ki.2:11; 6:17; Hab.3:8; Zech.1:8;
Rev.9:16*,17; 19:14
[*NIV translates as 'mounted troops']

iii.   A SIMILE for the wilfulness and stubbornness of sinners.
Ps.32:9; Pro.26:3; Jer.5:8*; 8:6
[*NIV translates as 'stallions']

iv.   A SYMBOL for the agents of God who carry out his decrees in the world's history.
Zech.6:2-6;
Rev.6:2-8

Host of heaven   See under 'Stars'.

House, Household   i.   A METAPHOR for the body which is the dwelling place of a person's soul and of the Holy Spirit in the case of Christians.
Ecc.12:3;
Matt.12:44; Lk.11:24; 2 Cor.5:1

ii.   A METAPHOR for one's family (including any servants), or for one's descendants, or one's tribe, nation or people, or for one's fellow believers (the 'household of faith').
Gen.18:19; Ex.2:1; Lev.10:6;
Num.17:8; Deut.14:26;
Josh.24:15; Judg.8:35[AV only];
2 Sam.9:1; 1 Ki.2:24[AV only];
1 Chr.10:6; Ps.98:3; Pro.12:7;
Isa.31:2; Ezek.2:5; Hos.1:4;
Amos 1:4; Zech.12:7;
Matt.13:57; Mk.3:25; Lk.1:33;
Jn.4:53; Acts 11:14; Rom.16:10;
1 Tim.3:12, etc.

iii.   A METAPHOR for one's circumstances or living

conditions, e.g. 'the house of bondage'.
AV only - Ex.13:3; Deut.5:6;
6:12; 7:8; 8:14; 13:5,10;
Josh.24:17; Judg.6:8; Job 30:23;
Jer.34:13; Mic.6:4;
AV and NIV - Ecc.7:2

iv. A METAPHOR for one's wealth or possessions, including slaves and livestock.
Gen.39:5; 2 Sam.12:8;
2 Ki.20:13[AV only]; Ps.36:8;
49:11; Pro.19:14; Song.8:7;
Zech.5:4;
Matt.12:29; 13:52; Mk.3:27;
Lk.11:21

v. A METAPHOR for a temple. The symbolic dwelling-place of God amongst people. Also used for the temples of idols.
AV only - 1 Ki.6:22; 2 Ki.10:21;
2 Chr.7:1; Ezra 5:8; Neh.2:8;
Isa.6:4; Ps.23:6;
AV and NIV - Gen.28:17;
Ex.23:19; Deut.23:18; Josh.6:24;
Judg.18:31; 1 Chr.17:4; Jer.7:30;
Lam.2:7; Joel 1:9;
Matt.12:4, etc.

vi. A METAPHOR for one's character or reputation, or for one's influence on others, whether it be for good or evil.
Pro.2:18; 5:8; 7:27; 9:1; 21:12;
Song.2:4*; 3:4; 8:2; Isa.22:18;
Matt.5:15; 7:24-27; Lk.6:48,49
[*NIV translates as 'hall']

vii.   A METAPHOR for the church,
       i.e. those who together
       acknowledge the Lordship of
       Christ.
       Num.12:7;
       Matt.10:25; Mk.13:34,35;
       Eph.2:19; 2 Tim.2:20; Heb.3:2,6;
       10:21; 1 Pet.2:5

House of the Lord   See under 'Temple'.

Hurt   See under 'Wound(s)'.

Husband   A METAPHOR for Christ. He has given
                         himself to his church in a covenant of
                         love which cannot be broken. He is his
                         people's Lord, Protector and Provider.
                         See also under 'Marriage' and 'Wife'.
                         Isa.54:5; Jer.3:14; 2 Cor.11:2;
                         Rev.21:2

Incense   A SYMBOL or SIMILE for prayer. As
                         incense rises when burned, so do our
                         prayers ascend to God. As incense has a
                         pleasing aroma, so does prayer please
                         God when offered in the name of Christ.
                         However, this figure is also used for the
                         corrupt worship of idols: the context
                         must decide the meaning.
                         Ex.30:1-9; Lev.4:7; Num.7:14;
                         Deut.33:10; 1 Sam.2:28; 1 Ki.9:25;
                         1 Chr.6:49; 2 Chr.13:11; Neh.13:9;
                         Ps.141:2; Isa.1:13; Jer.1:16;
                         Ezek.6:4,13; Hos.2:13; Hab.1:16;
                         Mal.1:11;
                         Lk.1:9; Rev.5:8; 8:3,4, etc.

Iron   i.   A SIMILE for something hard,
                         unyielding, powerfully destruc-
                         tive or cruel, e.g. just as the

heavens would be impenetrable to the prayers of the Israelites who rebelled against God.
Lev.26:19; Deut.28:23,48; 33:25; Job 40:18; Ps.2:9; 107:10,16; 149:8; Isa.45:2; Jer.1.18; Dan.2:33; Amos 1:3; Mic.4:13; Rev.2:27; 9:9; 12:5; 19:15

ii.   A SYMBOL of economic wealth.
Deut.8:9; Isa.60:17; Ezek.27:12,19; Rev.18:12

iii.   A METAPHOR for discernment or understanding.
Pro.27:17

iv.   A METAPHOR for stubbornness.
Isa.48:4

Israel, Israelites   The nation of Israel as the chosen people of God in the Old Testament was in that sense a TYPE of the church, i.e. those who are born of the Spirit into the kingdom of God.
See also under 'Jew'.
Gen.49:24; Ex.4:22; Lev.9:1; Num.23:23; Deut.10:12; Ps,73:1; 149:2; Isa.44:21-23; Jer.31:27-37; Ezek.37:11; Hos.14:5; Matt.2:6; Lk.24:21; Jn.1:31; Rom.9:6; 11:26; 1 Cor.10:18; Gal.6:16; Heb.8:8,10; Rev.7:4; 21:12, etc.

Jackals   See under 'Fox'.

Jars of clay   See under 'Earth(ly)'.

Jerusalem	i.	Under the old covenant, Jerusalem, as the place where God dwelt among his people, was a TYPE of the church. See also under 'City' and 'Zion'. 2 Sam.15:29; 1 Ki.11:13; Ps.51:18; 137:5; Song.6:4; Isa.40:9; 52:9; Jer.3:17; Joel 3:17; Zech.1:14; Mal.3:4; Gal.4:26; Rev.3:12; 21:2,10, etc.
	ii.	A SYMBOL and a TYPE for a false church, i.e. those who profess to be true believers but fail to seek God in the right way. 2 Ki.21:12; 1 Chr.24:18; Isa.1:1; Jer.26:18; Lam.1:8; Ezek.16:2; Gal.4:25, etc.

Jew

A METAPHOR for a true worshipper of God, not necessarily of Jewish descent. See also under 'Israel'.
Zech.8:23
Rom.2:28,29

Joined

See under 'Yoke(d)'.

Joseph

He was the son of Jacob and Rachel and in his rejection, suffering and subsequent exaltation for the deliverance of his people was a TYPE of Christ.
Gen.chs.30-50; Ps.105:17, etc.

Joshua

He was the son of Nun and was a TYPE of Christ as he led God's people into the promised land. 'Joshua' is the Hebrew equivalent of 'Jesus' which means 'Jehovah saves'.
Ex.17:13,14; Num.14:30; 27:18;
Deut.1:38; 34:9; Josh.chs.1-24, etc.

Jubilee		A TYPE of the gospel in which our spiritual slavery is ended and by which we receive our heavenly inheritance in Christ. Lev.25:9-13,28,30-33,54; 27:17,18, 21,24; Num.36:4, cf. Lk.4:19
Keys	i.	A SYMBOL for the gospel of Christ, i.e. the means by which we may enter God's kingdom. (Peter preached first to Jews and then to Romans and so used the keys of the gospel to open the kingdom for Jews and Gentiles). Matt.16:19; Lk.11:52
	ii.	A SYMBOL for authority, especially for the absolute authority of Christ over all things including the powers of death and hell. Isa.22:22; Rev.1:18; 3:7; 9:1; 20:1
Lamb(s) See also under 'Sheep'	i.	A SYMBOL for Christ which suggests his meekness and humility. As the main animal used for sacrifice, it foreshadowed Christ as the One who gave himself as a sacrifice for our sins. The sacrificial lamb was a clean animal which had to be without blemish and thus it also speaks of the holiness of Christ. The victory of Christ, in that it was accomplished through his humiliation and death, is an apparent contradiction. Therefore, we find that the SYMBOL of a lamb, in apocalyptic literature, is also frequently used as an appropriate

designation for the glorified, enthroned Christ in the book of Revelation.
Gen.22:7; Ex.12:3; Num.6:14;
1 Sam.7:9; Isa.53:7; Jer.11:19;
Ezek.46:13;
Jn.1:29,36; Acts 8:32;
Rev.5:6-13; 6:1,16; 7:9-17;
12:11; 13:8; 14:1-10; 15:3;
17:14; 19:7,9; 21:9-27; 22:3

ii.   A METAPHOR for believers, sometimes with young believers especially in mind.
Isa.5:17; 40:11;
Lk.10:3; Jn.21:15

iii. A SIMILE for those who are destined for slaughter under the judgment of God.
Isa.34:6; Jer.51:40; Ezek.39:18

iv.   A SIMILE for the false prophet.
Rev.13:11

Lamp(s), Lampstand   i.   A SYMBOL for the work of
See also under   Christ as a divine enlightener of
'Light'.   his people.
Ex.25:31; Num.8:2; 1 Ki.7:49;
Ps.132:17;
Heb.9:2

ii.   A SYMBOL for God's people as they bear witness to the truth of Christ.
Isa.62:1*; Zech.4:2,11;
Matt.5:15; 25:1-8; Mk.4:21;
Lk.8:16; Rev.1:12,13,20; 2:5;
11:4, etc.
[*NIV translates as 'torch']

iii. A METAPHOR for the Scriptures.
Ps.119:105: Pro.6:23

iv. A METAPHOR for one's spirit or life.
Job 18:6; 21:17; Ps.18:28; Pro.13:9; 20:20,27; 24:20

Land See under 'Earth(ly)'.

Land of Canaan As the forum for social and economic relationships and as Eden 'restored' for the old covenant people of God, the land of Canaan is a TYPE both of the fellowship of God's new covenant people and of the future new earth.
Ex.3:8; Num.13:27, etc. Deut.15:4; Ps.37:11, cf. Matt.5:5.

Lands See under 'World'

Lead (noun) A metal used as a SYMBOL to represent sin or sinning. Suggesting either sin's heaviness which hinders us from living for God as we ought, or its comparative worthlessness. Unlike silver or gold, lead is burned up in the furnace. In the same way, sin cannot endure the test of God's judgment as can true faith and the righteousness that Christ gives to those who trust in him.
Ex.15:10; Jer.6:29; Ezek.22:18,20; 27:12; Zech.5:7,8

Lead (verb) See under 'Walk(s)'.

Leaven A SYMBOL used to represent the influence of doctrines, teachings or

behaviour among people. Mostly in a bad sense of corrupt teachings but sometimes for the gospel as in Matt.13:33* and Lk.13:21*.
Ex.12:15-39*; 13:3*,7*; Lev.2:11*; 6:17*; 10:12*; 23:17*; Hos.7:4[AV only]; Amos 4:5;
Matt.13:33*; 16:6,11,12*; Mk.8:15*; Lk.12:2*; 13:21*; 1 Cor.5:6*,7*; Gal.5:9*
[*NIV translates as 'yeast']

Leaves

i. A SYMBOL representing human attempts to cover the shame and degradation of sin or, in other words, a man-made religion which is corrupt.
Gen.3:7
Matt.21:19; Mk.11:13

ii. A SYMBOL representing the gospel of Christ - that is, God's effective remedy for sin.
Rev.22:2

Leopard

i. An animal used as a SYMBOL to represent the qualities of speed and ferocity.
Isa.11:6; Jer.5:6; Dan.7:6; Hos.13:7; Hab.1:8;
Rev.13:2

ii. The leopard's spots are used as a SIMILE for sin, which is an inborn part of a sinner's nature and cannot be removed except by the grace of God. It is habitual sin and its hardening, enslaving effects that are especially in mind.
Jer.13:23

Leper(s), Leprous
Leprosy

A TYPE of sin. What leprosy does to the body, so sin does to the soul. It disfigures, it cuts us off from others, it bars from God's presence and finally it brings death.
Ex.4:6; Lev.13:2-46; Num.12:10; Deut.24:8; 2 Sam.3:29; 2 Ki.5:3; 2 Chr.26:20; Matt.8:2; Mk.1:40; Lk.5:12,13, etc.

Light(s)

i. A SYMBOL used to represent spiritual truth and holiness. Used especially of Christ and of believers, who bear witness to him by their holy lives and by declaring the truth of the gospel. Sometimes used more generally for the voice of conscience within every person (e.g. Jn.1:4,9).
See also under 'Stars'.
Lev.24:2; Num.8:2; 2 Sam.23:4; Job 24:13; Ps.27:1; 119:105; Pro.4:18; Isa.9:2; Dan.2:22; Mic.7:9; Matt.4:16; 5:14; Lk.2:32; Jn.1:4,9; 3:19; 8:12; Acts 13:47; Rom.2:19; 2 Cor.4:4,6; Eph.5:8; Col.1:12; 1 Thess.5:5; 1 Tim.6:16; 1 Pet.2:9; 1 Jn.1:5,7; Rev.21:23, etc.

ii. A METAPHOR for something being revealed.
See also under 'Darkness' and 'Lamp'.
Zeph.3:5[AV only]; 1 Cor.4:5; Eph.5:13; 2 Tim.1:10

Lightning(s)   A SYMBOL used to describe God's
                                    holiness and wrath which he often
                                    displays in an instant. Also used for the
                                    awesome holiness and swiftness of
                                    God's angels.
                                    See also under 'Lights'.
                                    Ex.19:16; 20:18; 2 Sam.22:15;
                                    Job 37:3; Ps.18:14; 77:18; 97:4;
                                    Ezek.1:13,14; Dan.10:6; Hos.6:5[NIV
                                    only]; Zech.9:14;
                                    Matt.24:27; 28:3; Lk.10:18;
                                    Rev.4:5; 8:5; 11:19; 16:18

Lily(ies)   A SYMBOL for the beauty of the church
                                    as viewed by Christ as he sees her washed
                                    and sanctified by his blood.
                                    1 Ki.7:19,26; 2 Chr.4:5; Hos.14:5

Lion(s), Lioness   i.   An animal used as a SYMBOL to
                                    denote the power, strength and/or
                                    courage:
                                    a. of God or of the Lord Jesus
                                       Christ
                                       Job 10:16; Isa.38:13;
                                       Jer.2:30; 25:38; 49:19;
                                       50:44; Lam.3:10; Hos.5:14;
                                       11:10; 13:7,8; Amos 3:4,8,12;
                                       Rev.5:5
                                    b. of God's people
                                       Gen.49:9; Num.24:9;
                                       Deut.33:20,22; 2 Sam.17:10
                                       Pro.28:1; Ezek.19:2,6;
                                       Mic.5:8
                                    c. of the cherubim
                                       Ezek.1:10; 10:14;
                                       Rev.4:7; 10:3
                                    d. of those who are naturally strong
                                       1 Chr.12:8; Job 4:10,11;
                                       Ps.34:10; Isa.11:7; 21:8[AV
                                       only]; 65:25

ii.   A SYMBOL used to represent royalty or civil power.
1 Ki.10:19,20; 2 Chr.9:18,19; Pro.19:12; 20:2

iii.   A SYMBOL used to represent the vicious and ruthless enemies of God and his people. Including wicked people, fallen angels and Satan.
Ps.7:2; 10:9; 17:12; 22:13,21; 35:17; 57:4; 58:6; 91:13; Song.4:8; Isa.5:29; 15:9; 35:9; Jer.2:15; 4:7; 5:6; 12:8; 50:17; 51:38; Ezek.22:25; Dan.7:4; Joel 1:6; Nah.2:11,12; Zeph.3:3; Zech.11:3; 2 Tim.4:17; 1 Pet.5:8; Rev.9:8,17; 13:2

Liquor   See under 'Wine'.

Living creatures   A METONYMY for the highest angelic
or Living ones   beings who live in the immediate presence of God, to serve and worship him. Their outstanding feature is the astounding vigour of their life.
Ezek.1:5-15;
Rev.4:6-9*; 5:6*,8*,11*,14*; 6:1,3,5,7; 7:11*
[*AV translates as 'beasts']

Locusts   i.   The devastation caused by these insects makes them a very apt SYMBOL to denote the ravages caused by sin or judgment on sin and by hosts of demons.
Joel 1:4; 2:25;
Rev.9:3,7

| | ii. | A SIMILE for a panic-stricken crowd desperately trying to flee from God's judgments. Isa.33:4; Nah.3:15-17 |

ii. A SIMILE for a panic-stricken crowd desperately trying to flee from God's judgments.
Isa.33:4; Nah.3:15-17

iii. A SIMILE for one's weakness and vulnerability apart from God.
Ps.109:23

Lucifer   See under 'Star'.

Mammon   See under 'World'.

Man child   See under 'Son(s)'.

Manna   A TYPE of Christ. As the Israelites were miraculously fed on their journeys through the desert, so too, believers nourish their souls by faith in Christ.
See also under 'Bread'.
Ex.16:15[AV only],31,33,35;
Num.11:6,7,9; Deut.8:3,16; Josh.5:12;
Neh.9:20; Ps.78:24;
Jn.6:31,49; Heb.9:4; Rev.2:17

Marriage, Married   A SYMBOL used to describe the enduring, intimate and loving relationship between Christ and his people.
See also under 'Bride', 'Husband' and 'Wife'.
Isa.62:4,5;
Matt.22:2*,4*,9*; 25:10;
Rev.19:7*,9*;
[*NIV translates as 'wedding']

Measure(d)   i.   When food or drink are said to
Measuring   be measured, this is sometimes a METAPHOR for a drought or a famine.
Ezek.4:11,16*;
Rev.6:6+

[*NIV translates as 'rationed';
+NIV translates as 'quart']

ii.   A METAPHOR for ownership. Often used for that which belongs to God (e.g. the church) and is therefore set apart as holy to him.
Jer.31:39; Ezek.chs.40,41,42;
Zech.2:1,2;
Rev.11:1,2; 21:15-17

Meat   i.   A SYNECDOCHE for the observance of Jewish ceremonial laws which Christ's coming made obsolete.
Rom.14:15*,20+; Col.2:16*;
1 Tim.4:3+; cf.Heb.9:10; 13:9
[*NIV translates as 'eat';
+NIV translates as 'food']

ii.   A METAPHOR for solid biblical teaching.
1 Cor.3:2*; cf.Heb.5:12,14
[*NIV translates as 'food']

iii.   A METAPHOR for the deep satisfaction that comes from serving God.
See also under 'Manna'.
Jn.4:32*,34*
[*NIV translates as 'food']

Megiddo   See 'Armageddon'.

Melchizedek   The royal priest to whom Abram offered gifts. A TYPE of Christ as the high priest superior to all other high priests. See Heb.7 for details.
Gen.14:18; Ps.110:4;
Heb.5:6,10; 6:20; 7:1-21

Mercy Seat	The covering of the ark of the covenant which was sprinkled with the blood of the sacrifice. A TYPE of Christ, in that he shields his people from the penalty of God's laws which they have broken, or from the wrath of God which his blood turns aside. Ex.25:17,20,22*; 26:34*; 37:6*; 40:20*; Lev.16:2*; Num.7:89* [*NIV translates as 'cover' or 'atonement cover']

Milk

i.   A TYPE of the rich blessings to be enjoyed by believers under the new covenant.
See also under 'Honey'.
Deut.32:14; Song.4:11; 5:1; Isa.7:22; 55:1; 60:16; 66:11[AV only]; Joel 3:18

ii.   A METAPHOR for the most basic teachings of Scripture, i.e. the first things new believers learn.
1 Cor.3:2; Heb.5:12,13; 1 Pet.2:2

iii.   A SIMILE for whiteness and beauty. This may mean external beauty, or it may also refer to inner beauty of spirit, i.e. holiness.
Gen.49:12; Song.5:12; Lam.4:7

Millstone

i.   A SYMBOL used to represent one's work, i.e. how one earns one's daily bread. Thus, the removal of the millstone represents a terrible loss.
Deut.24:6; Isa.47:2; Jer.25:10; Rev.18:21

	ii.	A millstone being cast into the sea is a vivid picture of a final and irrevocable judgment. Matt.18:6; Mk.9:42; Lk.17:2; Rev.18:21
Mire, Miry (or Mud)	i.	A SYMBOL for sin. Mire is deceitful in that it can appear to be solid ground. It is fatal in that it can slowly suck its victim under. It makes one dirty and polluted. All these are true of sin. Ps.40:2; 69:2,14; Isa.57:20; 2 Pet.2:22
	ii.	A METAPHOR for a state of hopelessness and despair, e.g. suffering a humiliating defeat at the hand of one's enemies. 2 Sam.22:43; Job 30:19; Isa.10:6; Mic.7:10; Zech.10:5
	iii.	A SIMILE for worthlessness. Zech.9:3* [*NIV translates as 'dirt']
Mirror		See under 'Glass'.
Monster		See under 'Dragon'.
Morning Star		One of the titles of the Lord Jesus Christ. At certain times of the year the planet Venus is the brightest object in the sky just prior to the dawning of the day. So Jesus Christ brought in the light of the gospel age. 2 Pet.1:19; Rev.2:28; 22:16
Morning Stars		A METAPHOR for the angels. Job 38:7

Mount, Mountain(s)   i.   A SYMBOL for the meeting place
                                    between God and people where
                                    God reveals himself and where
                                    people respond in worship.
                                    Gen.22:2; 31:54*; Ex.18:5;
                                    19:18; 24:16; 31:18; Deut.1:6;
                                    Judg.5:5; 1 Ki.19:8; Ps.48:1;
                                    133:3; 144:5; Isa.10:32; 27:13;
                                    30:29; Ezek.34:13,14; 35:8;
                                    36:1,4,8; 37:22; 39:2;
                                    Joel 3:18; Amos 9:13; Zech.6:1;
                                    Matt.17:1; Rev.21:10, etc.
                                    [*NIV translates as 'hill country']

                            ii.   A SYMBOL for a particular
                                    dispensation, either of the law or
                                    of the gospel, the nation of Israel
                                    or of the church.
                                    Ps.72:16*; Song.4:6; Isa.2:2,3;
                                    25:6,7,10; 65:9; Jer.50:6;
                                    Ezek.17:22,23; Dan.2:35,45;
                                    Mic.4:1,2; Hab.3:3;
                                    Gal.4:24,25; Heb.12:18,20
                                    [*NIV translates as 'hills']

                            iii.   A SYMBOL for a place of refuge
                                    and security which, if a false
                                    refuge, can be overturned.
                                    Sometimes used of God, in whom
                                    we have true security for eternity.
                                    Ps.11:1; 30:7; 36:6; 46:2,3;
                                    65:6; 90:2; 104:6; 125:2;
                                    Isa.22:5; 54:10; 64:1,3;
                                    Jer.4:24; Ezek.38:20; Hos.10:8;
                                    Mic.1:4; Nah.1:5; Hab.3:6,10;
                                    Matt.24:16; Mk.13:14; Lk.21:21;
                                    23:30; Rev.6:15,16; 16:20

                            iv.   A METAPHOR for obstacles or
                                    barriers. Especially those that

come between God and his people,
i.e. our sins.
Song.2:8,17*; 8:14; Isa.40:4;
49:11;
Matt.17:20; 21:21; Mk.11:23;
Lk.3:5
[*NIV translates as 'hills']

v. Following (i), when religion
became corrupt, mountain tops
became the scene of the sinful
worship of idols.
Deut.12:2; Isa.57:7*; 65:7;
Jer.3:6*,23; Ezek.6:2,3,13; 18:6,
11,15; 22:9; 34:6; Hos.4:13
[*NIV translates as 'hill']

vi. A METAPHOR for a king, a
government or a nation and its
power.
Ps.72:3; 83:14; 114:4,6;
Isa.41:15; Jer.46:18; 51:25;
Ezek.36:1-6; Obad.8,21;
Zech.4:7; 14:4,5;
Rev.17:9*
[*NIV translates as 'hills']

vii. A METAPHOR for this sinful
world in its lofty pride and vanity.
2 Ki.19:23; Song.4:8; Isa.37:24

viii. A SYMBOL for the place where
messages are openly proclaimed
to all, e.g. for the public
proclamation of the gospel.
Isa.13:2*; 18:3; 40:9; 42:11;
52:7; Nah.1:15
[*NIV translates as 'hilltops']

ix.   A SYMBOL for a vantage point
       from which one can see for great
       distances.
       Deut.32:49,50;
       Matt.4:8; Lk.4:5*
       [*NIV translates as 'high place']

x.   A METONYMY for the world as
       a part of God's creation.
       Mountains arc often personified as
       though they were offering praise
       to God.
       Deut.32:22; Ps.90:2; 148:9
       Pro.8:25; Isa.40:12; 44:23;
       49:13; 55:12; Amos 4:13;
       Mic.6:1,2

xi.   A METAPHOR for a barren and
       infertile place.
       Isa.30:25

xii.   A METAPHOR for a great
       abundance.
       Ps.76:4

Myrtle Tree(s)   A SYMBOL for the Lord's people who,
                        by his grace, are made sweet and
                        beautiful in spirit.
                        Isa.41:19: 55:13; Zech.1:8,10,11

Naked(ness)   A SYMBOL used to describe the shame
                        and degradation of sinful human nature
                        when exposed to the light of God's
                        omniscience and holiness.
                        Gen.3:7,10,11; Ex.20:26; 28:42[AV
                        only]; 1 Sam.20:30[AV only];
                        Job 26:6; Isa.47:3; Lam.1:8;
                        Ezek.16:8,36,37; 23:10,18,29;
                        Hos.2:3,9; Nah.3:5;
                        2 Cor.5:3; Heb.4:13[AV only];
                        Rev.3:17,18; 16:15; 17:16

Name(s)	Names in Scripture are very often metaphorical descriptions of the character, office, reputation, works, etc. of the person, e.g. 'in my name' means 'because of who I am'. This is especially so in the case of the names of God. Names in Scripture may also refer to the descendants or followers of a person, e.g. Christians are called after the name of Christ.

Gen.11:4; Ex.34:14; Deut.7:24;
Josh.23:7; 2 Sam.6:2; 1 Ki.14:21;
Ezra 5:1; Ps.20:1; Pro.18:10;
Isa.56:5; Jer.14:14; Ezek.20:9;
Zech.6:12;
Matt.10:41[AV only]; Lk.21:8;
Jn.14:13; Acts 9:15; Rom.9:17;
Rev.2:3; 19:12,16, etc.

Night

i. A METAPHOR for unbelief and ignorance of God (i.e. a lack of spiritual 'light').
Jn.11:10; Rom.13:12;
1 Thess.5:2,5; 2 Pet,3:10[AV only]; Rev.21:25; 22:5

ii. A METAPHOR for a period of affliction or persecution. Sometimes used for the experience of a believer when the Lord seems to be far away.
Ps.30:5; Isa.21:12; Lam.1:2;
Joel 1:13; Mic.3:6

iii. A METAPHOR for death.
Jn.9:4

Not clean   See 'Unclean'.

Oak(s)   i.   A tree often associated with idol
                            worship and therefore sometimes
                            used as a figure for false worship
                            and its devotees.
                            Isa.1:29,30; 2:13; Ezek.6:13;
                            Hos.4:13; Zech.11:2

                    ii.   A SIMILE for the nation of Israel.
                            Isa.6:13

                    iii.   A SIMILE for strength.
                            Amos 2:9

Oil   i.   A SYMBOL used to denote the
                            grace of God either his common
                            grace in some special blessing or
                            giving gifts for some particular
                            work, or for his special grace in the
                            gift of the Holy Spirit to his
                            people.
                            See also under 'Anointing'.
                            Ex.25:6; 27:20; 30:24,25;
                            Lev.14:15-18,29; 24:2; Num.4:9;
                            Deut.32:13; 33:24; 1 Sam.10:1;
                            16:1,13; 1 Ki.1:39; 17:12,14,16;
                            2 Ki.4:2,6,7; 9:1,3; Job 29:6;
                            Ps.23:5; 104:15; 109:18; 141:5;
                            Pro.21:20; Isa.61:3;
                            Ezek.16:18,19; Zech.4:12;
                            Matt.25:3,4,8

                    ii.   A SYNECDOCHE for the good
                            produce of the earth. One of the
                            items required by God in the old
                            covenant tithes. Therefore this is
                            closely connected with (i) above.
                            Lev.2:1-6; Num.6:15; 15:4,6;
                            18:12; Deut.7:13; 11:14; 12:17;
                            14:23; 18:4; 28:51; 1 Chr.9:29;
                            12:40; 2 Chr.2:10,15; 11:11;

		32:28; Ezra 6:9; Neh.10:37,39; 13:5,12; Ps.104:15; Jer.31:12; 41:8; Ezek.27:17; Hag.1:11
	iii.	A SIMILE for flattering words. Ps.55:21; Pro.5:3
	iv.	A SYNECDOCHE for luxury items used for consumption or for trade. Pro.21:17; Hos.12:1; Rev.6:6; 18:13
	v.	A SIMILE for stagnation. Ezek.32:14
Olive(s)	i.	A SYMBOL used to describe spiritual health and fruitfulness. 1 Ki.6:23,31-33; Ps.52:8; 128:3; Zech.4:3,12; Rev.11:4
	ii.	A SYMBOL for the nation of Israel, which is also a TYPE of the church. See also under 'Israel'. Isa.17:6; 24:13; Jer.11:16; Hos.14:6; Rom.11:17.24
Oven	i.	A SYMBOL used to describe God's burning anger and wrath against all sin. Ps.21:9*; Mal.4:1*; Matt.6:30+; Lk.12:28+ [*NIV translates as 'furnace'; +NIV translates as 'fire']
	ii.	A SIMILE for the burning lusts that rage in the hearts of the wicked. Hos.7:4,6,7

iii.   A SIMILE for the fever that
accompanies famine.
See also under 'Furnace'.
Lam.5:10

Ox(en)   A SYMBOL for those who labour
mightily in the Lord's service. Usually
applied to pastors or elders.
Deut.22:10; 25:4;
1 Cor.9:9; 1 Tim.5:18

Palm branches   A SYMBOL for the celebration of a
triumph.
Jn.12:13; Rev.7:9 [cf.Neh.8:15]

Palm tree(s)   A SYMBOL used to describe the
strength, faithfulness and moral
uprightness of a believer's nature.
1 Ki.6:29-35; 7:36; 2 Chr.3:5;
Ps.92:12; Ezek.40:16; 41:18,19

Passover   The feast celebrating the deliverance of
the Israelites from their slavery in Egypt
through the slaying of lambs and the
application of their blood to the door-
frames of the houses. This is a TYPE of
the deliverance of Christians from the
slavery of sin through the blood of Christ.
Ex.12:11-49; Num.9:2-6; Deut.16:1-6;
Josh.5:10; 2 Ki.23:21-23;
Ezra 6:19,20; Ezek.45:21
Lk.22:15; 1 Cor.5:7; Heb.11:28, etc.

Pastors   See under 'Shepherd(s)'.

Pasture   A METAPHOR for God's care of and
provision for his people.
See also under 'Sheep'.
Ps.23:2; 74:1; 79:13; 95:7; 100:3;
Jer.23:1; 25:36; Ezek.34:14,18

Pearl(s)　　　　　　i.　　A METAPHOR for the precious truths of Christ's gospel.
Matt.7:6; 13:45,46[AV only]; Rev.21:21

　　　　　　　　　ii.　　A METONYMY for the superficial attractiveness of this world's riches expressed by extravagant display of wealth.
1 Tim.2:9; Rev.17:4; 18:12,16

Pig　　　　　　See under 'Swine'.

Pillar(s)　　　　　　A SYMBOL used to describe either an individual believer or the church as a firm maintainer of the truth and reliability of the Scriptures.
Jer.1:18;
Gal.2:9; 1 Tim.3:15; Rev.3:12

Pillar of cloud
Pillar of fire
　　　　　　A TYPE of Christ and his Word. As this pillar guided and protected the Israelites through the desert of Sinai so, too, Jesus guides and protects his people through their lives on this earth to bring them safely to heaven.
See also under 'Cloud' and 'Fire'.
Ex.13:21,22; 14:24; 40:36,37;
Num.9:17; 10:11; 12:5; Deut.1:33;
31:15; Neh.9:12

Pit(s)　　　　　　A METAPHOR for the place of deep trouble or for death or for the depths of hell.
Job 17:16(AV only); 33:18; Ps.9:15;
40:2; 119:85*; Pro.1:12; 23:27;
Isa.14:15; 24:17,18; Lam.4:20+;
Ezek.19:4; 32:23; Zech.9:11;
Rev.9:1**,2**,11**; 11:7**; 17:8**;
20:1**,3**, etc.

[*NIV translates as 'pitfalls';
+NIV translates as 'traps';
**NIV translates as 'abyss']

Pitfalls	See under 'Pit(s)'.
Plagues	See under 'Wound'.
Plain	See under 'Valley'.
Plant (noun)	See under 'Grass'.
Planted	See under 'Plough(ed)'.

Plough(ed)
Ploughing

i. A METAPHOR for a severe discipline.
Ps.129:3; Jer.26:18; Hos.10:11; Mic.3:12

ii. A METAPHOR for the work of the gospel.
Lk.9:62; 1 Cor.9:10

iii. A METAPHOR for a life of sin.
Job 4:8; Hos.10:13*
[*NIV translates as 'planted']

Plumbline

A METAPHOR or SYMBOL for God's holy commandments by which the correctness of our lives is measured.
Amos 7:7,8

Poison

i. A METAPHOR or SIMILE for malicious speech.
Ps.58:4*; 140:3;
Rom.3:13; Jas.3:8
[*NIV translates as 'venom']

ii. A METAPHOR for the bitter experience of being disciplined by God.

Deut.32:24*; Job 6:4
[*NIV translates as 'venom']

iii.   A METAPHOR for the bitter
fruits or results of sin.
Deut.32:33; Job 20:16

Poisoned water   See under 'Gall'.

Pollute
Pollution
   A METAPHOR for the way in which
sin and compromise with the world spoil
that which is intended to be holy.
See also under 'Adultery'.
Ex.20:25*; Num.35:33,34*;
2 Ki.23:16*; 2 Chr.36:14*;
Neh.7:64+; Ps.106:38**;
Isa.56:2**,6**; Jer.2:23*; 3:1*,2*;
7:30*; Ezek.4:14*; 14:11*;
20:30*,31*; 22:10+; Ezek.23:17,30*;
36:18; Hos.9:4+; Mic.2:10*; Zeph.3:1*;
Mal.1:7,12*
Acts 15:20; 21:28*; 2 Pet.2:20++
[*NIV translates as 'defile';
+NIV translates as 'unclean';
**NIV translates as 'desecrate';
++NIV translates as 'corruption']

Polluted   See under 'Unclean'.

Pomegranates   A TYPE of the fruit of the Spirit, perhaps
because of its many seeds, or because of
its sweetness.
See also under 'Fruit'.
Ex.28:33,34; 39:24-26; 1 Ki.7:18;
2 Ki.25:17; 2 Chr.3:16; Song.4:3,13;
6.7,11; 7:12; 8:2; Jer.52:22

Poor   i.   A METAPHOR for those who
consciously lack any true
righteousness of their own and

who are humbly dependent on
God.
1 Sam.2:8; Ps.34:6; 40:17;
69:29[AV only]; 70:5; 86:1;
109:22; Isa.66:2[AV only];
Matt.5:3

ii.   A METAPHOR for spiritual
        destitution in those who are not
        conscious of it.
        Rev.3:17

Potter   A METAPHOR for God who moulds the
                    characters of his people, e.g. through the
                    circumstances he places them in.
                    Isa.29:16; 45:9; 64:8; Jer.18:4,6;
                    Rom.9:21

Potter's jar   See under 'Potter's vessel'.

Potter's vessel   A TYPE representing God in his terrible
                    fury breaking the nations of the earth
                    because in their sinfulness and pride they
                    have no value to him and are an offence
                    to him.
                    Ps.2:9*; Isa.30:14*; Jer.19:11+;
                    Rev.2:27*
                    [*NIV translates as 'pottery';
                    +NIV translates as 'potter's jar']

Pottery   See 'Potter's vessel'.

Prison   i.   A METAPHOR for the spiritual
Prisoner   captivity in which unbelievers are
                        held by sin and by Satan.
                        Isa.42:7,22; 61:1;
                        Lk.4:18; Gal.3:23

                ii.   A METAPHOR for hell.
                        Isa.24:22;
                        Matt.5:25; Lk.12:58; 1 Pet.3:19;
                        Rev.20:7

iii.   A METAPHOR for the affliction which believers sometimes experience.
Ps.142:7

Promiscuity   See under 'Fornication'.

Prostitute   See under 'Fornication'.

Purify   See under 'Clean(se)'.

Purple   The colour which is sometimes used to SYMBOLIZE royalty. For example, the purple used in the tabernacle SYMBOLIZES the kingship of Christ.
Ex.25:4; 26:1; 39:3; Num.4:13;
Judg.8:26; 2 Chr.2:7,14; 3:14;
Song.3:10; 7:5*; Ezek.27:7;
Mk.15:17; Lk.16:19; Jn.19:2;
Rev.17:4; 18:12,16, etc.
[*NIV translates as 'tapestry']

Quart   See under 'Measure'.

Race   A METAPHOR for the Christian life which demands our full commitment and self-discipline in order to finish.
See also under 'Running'.
1 Cor.9:24; Heb.12:1

Rain   i.   A SYMBOL used to describe the refreshing blessings God sends on his people through the ministry of his Word and other means of grace.
Deut.32:2; 2 Sam.23:4;
Job 29:23; Ps.72:6; 84:6;
Hos.6:3; 10:12*;
[*NIV translates as 'showers']

ii.   A SYMBOL used to describe
        destructive judgments sent on the
        earth.
        Gen.7:4; Ex.9:33;
        1 Sam.12:17,18; Pro.28:3;
        Isa.4:6; Jer.10:13; 51:16;
        Ezek.38:22;
        Matt.7:25,27

iii.   A SYMBOL of the blessing of
        God on his people sometimes
        through his servants.
        Ps.68:9*; Ezek.22:24; Zech.10:1;
        [*NIV translates as 'showers']

Rainbow   The SYMBOL of God's faithfulness to
                   his covenant, thus guaranteeing that all
                   his promises will be fulfilled.
                   Gen.9:13; Ezek.1:28;
                   Rev.4:3; 10:1

Ram(s)   i.   An animal used for sacrifice under
                   the old covenant and thus a TYPE
                   of the Lord Jesus Christ.
                   See also under 'Lamb'.
                   Gen.15:9; 22:13;
                   Ex.29:15,16*,22,32; Lev.8:21,22;
                   9:2,4; 19:21; Num.5:8; 15:11;
                   1 Sam.15:22; 1 Chr.29:21;
                   Ezra 6:9,17; 10:19; Isa.1:11;
                   Ezek.43:23,25; 45:24; Mic.6:7

             ii.   A SYMBOL of the Medo-Persian
                   empire.
                   Dan.8:3-20

Ramparts   See under 'Tower(s)'.

Rationed   See under 'Measure'.

Reap(s), Reaping, Reapers	i.	A METAPHOR used either for the rewards of a righteous life or for the bitter results of a life of sin. The context must decide the meaning. See also under 'Harvest'. Job 4:8; Ps.126:5; Pro.22:8; Jer.12:13; Hos.8:7; 10:12,13; 1 Cor.9:11; 2 Cor.9:6; Gal.6:7-9
	ii.	A METAPHOR for the angels who will be used by God in the final judgment. Isa.17:5; Rev.14:15,16* [*NIV translates as 'harvested']
Red	i.	The colour associated with shed blood. Therefore, the rams' skins dyed red used in the tabernacle TYPIFIED the death of Christ. See also under 'Blood'. Ex.25:5; 26:14; 35:7,23; 36:19; 39:34; Num.19:2
	ii.	The colour sometimes used to SYMBOLIZE war and other deadly judgments. Isa.63:2; Nah.2:3; Zech.1:8; 6:2; Rev.6:4
	iii.	The colour sometimes used to SYMBOLIZE sin and evil. Isa.1:18 Rev.12:3
Reflection		See under 'Glass'.
River(s)	i.	A SYMBOL representing the grace of God flowing from him to his people.

Ps.36:8; 46:4; 78:16; 105:41;
Isa.30:25; 32:2*; 33:21; 41:18;
43:19*,20*; 48:18; 66:12;
Jer.17:8*; Ezek.47:5,9;
Jn.7:38*; Rev.22:1,2
[*NIV translates as 'streams']

ii.   A METAPHOR for a deep trial.
       Isa.43:2; 47:2*
       [*NIV translates as 'streams'].
       See also under 'Flood'.

iii.   A SYMBOL for the resources of
       strength and prosperity of an
       individual or nation.
       2 Ki.19:24*; Job 29:6*; Ps.1:3*;
       89:25; Song.5:12*; Isa.8:7;
       11:15; 19:5,6+; 32:2*; 37:25*;
       42:15; 44:27*; Jer.2:18; 17:8*;
       31:9*; 46:7,8; Ezek.29:3-10*;
       31:4*; 32:2*,14*; Nah.1:4;
       Hab.3:8
       Rev.8:10; 16:4
       [*NIV translates as 'streams';
       +NIV translates as 'canals']

iv.   A METAPHOR for a copious
       abundance.
       Job 20:17; Ps.119:136*;
       Lam.2:18; Mic.6:7
       [*NIV translates as 'streams']

v.   The phrase 'the river' is often used
       as a METAPHOR for either the
       Nile or the Euphrates.
       Gen.31:21; 36:37; 41:1[AV only];
       Ex.1:22; Josh.24:15[NIV only];
       1 Ki.4:21; Ezra 4:10[AV only];
       Ps.72:8; Mic.7:12[AV only];
       Zech.9:10

| | vi. | Rushing rivers are a SYMBOL of the fury of ungodly nations. Jer.46:7,8 |

Robe(s) i. A SYMBOL for some particular office, e.g. of the high priest or of a king.
Gen.49:11; Ex.28:4,31-34; 29:5; 39:22-26; Lev.8:7; 1 Ki.22:10,30; Esth.6:8-11; 8:15; Ps.45:8; 93:1; 133:2; Isa.6:1; 61:10; 63:1; Ezek.26:16; Jon.3:6; Rev.10:1; 19:13,16, etc.

ii. A SYMBOL used to represent holiness. Often for Christ's righteousness which is given to those who truly believe in him.
Job 29:14;
Mk.16:5; Lk.15:22;
Rev.6:11; 7:9,13,14
See also under 'Garment'.

Rock(s), (Stony) i. A METAPHOR for Christ who, like a rock, is dependable and unchanging in his love for undeserving sinners, while being an obstacle that trips up the wicked exposing their unbelief.
See also under 'Foundation'.
Gen.49:24; Ex.17:6;
Num.20:8-11; Deut.32:4,18,30,31; 1 Sam.2:2; 2 Sam.22:2; Ps.18:2; 40:2; 144:1; Isa.8:14; 44:8; Dan.2:34,35; Hab.1:12; Matt.7:24,25; Lk.6:48; Rom.9:33; 1 Cor.10:4; 1 Pet.2:8, etc.

ii. A METAPHOR for a leader who by the grace of God is enabled to

be a means of great blessing to others, even a basis for the fulfilment of God's redeeming purposes.
Isa.32:2;
Matt.16:18

iii.   A METAPHOR for an ancestor.
Isa.51:1

iv.   A METAPHOR for the church.
Zech.12:3

v.   A METAPHOR for unbelievers' stubborn prejudice against the gospel.
See also under 'Stones'.
Jer.5:3*; 23:29;
Matt.13:5,20; Mk.4:5,16;
Lk.8:6,13
[*NIV translates as 'stone']

vi.   A METAPHOR for those things unbelievers look to for security and help rather than God.
Num.24:21; Deut.32:31,37;
Isa.2:10,19,21; Jer.4:29; 48:28;
49:16; Obad.3;
Rev.6:15,16

Rod   A METAPHOR for an instrument of punishment or chastisement.
See also under 'Aaron's Rod', 'Measuring', 'Sceptre' and 'Staff'.
2 Sam.7:14; Job 9:34; 21:9; 23:4;
89:32; Pro.10:13; 13:24; 22:15;
Isa.10:5,15; 11:4; 30:32; Lam.3:1;
Ezek.7:10,11; 21:10; Mic.5:1; 6:9, etc.

Roll		See under 'Scroll'.
Root(s), Rooted	i.	A METAPHOR for the source of something or for someone's origins. Deut.29:18; Job 19:28; Isa.11:1,10; 14:29; 53:2; Mic.4:1 Matt.3:10; Lk.3:9; Rom.11:16-18; 15:12; Heb.12:15; Rev.5:5; 22:16
	ii.	A METAPHOR for being firm or established. Sometimes referring to a Christian's faith being founded in and sustained by God. 2 Ki.19:30; Job 5:3; 18:16; Ps.80:9; Pro.12:12; Isa.14:30; 27:6; 37:31; 40:24; Jer.12:2; 17:8; Ezek.17:6-9; 31:7; Dan.4:15,23,26; Hos.9:16; 14:5; Amos.2:9; Matt.13:6,21; 15:13; Mk.4:6,17; Lk.8:13; Eph.3:17; Col.2:7

Running, Runner

A SYMBOL for living the Christian life in which we are called to make every effort to follow after Christ.
See also under 'Race'.
1 Cor.9:24,26; Gal.2:2; 5:7;
Phil.2:16; Heb.12:1

Sackcloth

A SYMBOL used to represent deep sorrow and mourning because in Bible lands of olden times such sackcloth (a coarse piece of goat-hair or camel-hair cloth) was worn next to the skin during times of mourning. It may or may not be a godly sorrow leading to repentance.
Gen.37:34; Lev.11:32; 2 Sam.3:31;

1 Ki.20:31,32; 2 Ki.6:30;
1 Chr.21:16; Neh.9:1; Esth.4:1-4;
Job 16:15; Ps.30:11; Isa.3:24;
Jer.4:8; Lam.2:10; Ezek.7:18;
Dan.9:3; Joel 1:8,13; Amos 8:10;
Jon.3:5-8;
Matt.11:21; Lk.10:13; Rev.6:12;
11:3, etc.

Salt(y), Salted Saltiness	i.	A SYMBOL used to represent that which preserves from corruption and decay, especially in a moral, ethical or spiritual sense, e.g. the wholesome influence of Christians on the behaviour of a society. A covenant of salt means a lasting covenant. Ex.30:35; Lev.2:13; Num.18:19; 2 Ki.2:20,21; Ezek.16:4; 43:24; Matt.5:13; Mk.9:50; Lk.14:34; Col.4:6, etc.
	ii.	A SYMBOL used to represent judgment. Jer.17:6; Zeph.2:9; Mk.9:49
Salt water		A SYMBOL used to describe the pervasive influence of sin in people's speech and in their lives generally. Ezek.47:9-11; James 3:11,12
Sand	i.	A SIMILE for a vast and countless number. Gen.22:17; 32:12; Josh.11:4; Judg.7:12; 1 Sam.13:5; 2 Sam.17:11; 1 Ki.4:20,29; Job 6:3; 29:18; Ps.78:27; 139:18; Isa.10:22; 48:19;

Jer.15:8; 33:22; Hos.1:10;
Hab.1:9;
Rom.9:27; Heb.11:12; Rev.20:8

ii.   A METAPHOR for human effort and wisdom which cannot support us under the judgments of God. (Compare entry under 'Rock'). Matt.7:26

Sat down, Seated   An action SYMBOLIC of a task fully completed.
Heb.1:3; 10:12

Scales   See under 'Balance'.

Scapegoat   A TYPE of Christ, who suffered the terrible separation from God the Father when he bore our sins on the cross.
Lev.16:8,10,26
[See also Isa.53:6]

Scarlet   i.   The colour associated with the shedding of blood, and suggesting to us the atoning sacrifice of Christ.
Ex.25:4; 26:1-26; 28:5-33;
35:6-35; 36:8-37; 38:18,23;
39:1-29; Lev.14:4-52; Num.4:8;
19:6;

ii.   A colour associated with luxurious clothing, as worn by the very rich or by royalty.
2 Sam.1:24; Pro.31:21; Jer.4:30;
Nah.2:3;
Matt.27:28; Rev.17:4; 18:12,16

iii.   The colour sometimes used as a SYMBOLIC description of sin.

                                    See also under 'Red'.
                                    Isa.1:18;
                                    Rev.17:3

Scatter   See under 'Winnow'.

Sceptre(s)   A SYMBOL for the authority to rule,
                                    often used of Christ's authority.
                                    See also under 'Rod'.
                                    Gen.49:10; Num.21:18; 24:17;
                                    Ps.2:9; 45:6; 60:7; 108:8; 110:2;
                                    125:3; Isa.14:5; 30:31; Jer.48:17;
                                    Ezek.19:11,14; Amos 1:5,8;
                                    Zech.10:11;
                                    Rev.2:27; 12:5; 19:15

Scorpion   A METAPHOR for demons who are able
                                    to inflict people with the pain of guilt and
                                    remorse.
                                    Lk.10:19; Rev.9:3-10

Scoundrels   See under 'Belial'.

Scroll   i.   A SYMBOL for a particular
                                          message from God to certain
                                          people.
                                          Eze.2:9*; 3:1-3*;
                                          Rev.10:2-10+
                                          [*AV translates as 'roll';
                                          +AV translates as 'book']

                                    ii.   A METAPHOR for the decrees of
                                          God.
                                          Dan.12:4*; Zech.5:1,2+;
                                          Mal.3:16*;
                                          Rev.5:1-9*
                                          [*AV translates as 'book';
                                          +AV translates as 'roll']

Sea	i.	The bronze sea of the temple TYPIFIED the great reservoir of grace and cleansing that there is in Christ. 1 Ki.7:23-44; 2 Ki.16:17; 25:13,16; 2 Chr.4:2-15; Jer.52:20
	ii.	The sea of glass is a SYMBOL for the complete control of all things at the throne of God - utter calm results from his sovereignty. Rev.4:6
	iii.	A SYMBOL for the fury of the ungodly which is likened to the raging of a stormy sea. Isa.5:30; 17:12; Jer.6:23; 50:42; 51:42; Ezek.26:3; 27:34
	iv.	A SYMBOL for the peoples of the world in their state of rebellion against God. Isa.27:1; Dan.7:2,3; Lk.21:25; Rev.13:1; 21:1
	v.	A SIMILE for the restlessness of unbelievers. Isa.57:20; Jer.49:23; Jas.1:6; Jude 13
	vi.	A SYMBOL for something of very great dimensions. Job 11:9; Isa.11:9; Lam.2:13; Amos 9:3; Mic.7:19; Hab.2:14
	vii.	A METAPHOR for the depths of hell. Matt.18:6; Lk.17:2; Rev.18:21

viii.   The passage of the Israelites
        through the Red Sea TYPIFIED
        baptism and is therefore a
        SYMBOL for our initiation and
        consecration to Christ.
        Ex.14:2-29; 15:1-22;
        Josh.24:6,7; 2 Sam.22:16;
        Neh.9:9-11;
        Ps.18:15*; Isa.43:16; Nah.1:4;
        Zech.10:11;
        1Cor.10:1,2;Heb.11:29; Rev.15:2
        [*AV translates as 'waters']

Seal(s)   i.   A SYMBOL of someone or
                        something being secured or closed
                        up or kept secret.
                        Ps.40:9[NIV only]; Song.4:12;
                        Isa.29:11; Dan.8:26[NIV only];
                        12:9; Eph.4:30; Rev.5:1-9;
                        6:1-12; 8:1; 10:4; 20:3; 22:10

                ii.   A SYMBOL for someone or
                        something being confirmed as
                        genuine or true; a sign of
                        ownership. Often used of the
                        indwelling Holy Spirit whose
                        presence   confirms   the
                        genuineness of a believer as one
                        belonging to God.
                        Ex.28:11-36*; 39:6-30*;
                        Deut.29:12[NIV only]; Song.8:6;
                        Dan.9:24;
                        John 6:27; Rom.4:11; 1 Cor.9:2;
                        2 Cor.1:22; Eph.1:13;
                        2 Tim.2:19; Rev.7:3-8; 9:4
                        [*AV translates as 'signet']

Seed(s)	i.	A METAPHOR for Christ, referring to the line of descent of his human nature. Gen.3:15[AVonly]; 22:17,18[AV only]; Isa.6:13; Gal.3:16,19
	ii.	A METAPHOR for the Word of God. Ps.126:6; Ecc.11:6; Matt.13:3-19; Mk.4:3-31; Lk.8:5-15; 1 Cor.9:11[NIV only]; 1 Pet.1:23; 1 Jn.3:9
	iii.	A METAPHOR for believers. Matt.13:24,27,37,38; Mk.4:26,27 Gal.3:29
		See also under 'Fruit'.

Serpent

A SYMBOL used to describe the cunning and devious nature of Satan, the fallen angels and wicked people in general.
See also under 'Poison' and 'Dragon'.
Gen.3:1-14; 49:17; Deut.32:33*;
Job 20:14+,16+; Ps.91:13*; 140:3;
Isa.14:29; 27:1; 65:25; Jer.46:22;
51:34*;
2 Cor.11:3; Rev.12:9,14,15; 20:2
[*AV translates as 'dragons';
+AV translates as 'asps']

Seven(th)

A SYMBOL being the number often used to represent completeness or perfection. Often used in connection with God's involvement with the world either as Creator or as Redeemer. In Jewish thought the number seven was a

combination of three (the Godhead) and four (the number of the earth), thus embracing everything. Sometimes used for a complete period of time in God's plan of salvation (e.g. Dan.9:25-27*).
Gen.2:2; Ex.12:15; Lev.4:6; Num.19:4; Deut. 7:1; Josh.6:4; 1 Sam.10:8; Ezra 6:22; Ps.12:6; Pro.9:1; Isa.30:26; Dan.4:16; 9:27*; Zech.3:9;
Rev.1:4; 3:1; 21:9, etc.
[*AV translates as 'one week']

Shade, Shadow

i. A SYMBOL used to represent a pleasant shelter, hiding-place or refuge.
Judg.9:15; Job 34:22; Ps.17:8; 36:7; 57:1; 63:7; 80:10; 91:1; 121:5; Song.2:3; Isa.4:6; 16:3; 25:4,5; 30:2,3; 32:2; 34:15; 49:2; 51:16; Ezek.17:23; 31:6,12,17; Hos.4:13; 14:7; Mk.4:32

ii. A SYMBOL used to describe something frail or changeable, fleeting or temporary.
1 Chr.29:15; Job 8:9; 14:2; 17:7; Ps.102:11; 109:23; 144:4; Ecc.6:12;
Col.2:17; Heb.8:5; 10:1; Jas.1:17

iii. A METAPHOR for either physical or spiritual death.
See also under 'Darkness'.
Job 3:5; 10:21,22; 38:17; Ps.23:4; Isa.9:2; Matt.4:16; Lk.1:79

Sheaves   A SYMBOL used to point towards the
                        gathering of believers into heaven, or of
                        unbelievers into judgment.
                        See also under 'Harvest'.
                        Job 5:26*; Ps.126:6; Mic.4:12;
                        Zech.12:6
                        [*AV translates as 'shock']

Sheep   i.   A SIMILE for Christ, who meekly
                        resigned himself to the suffering
                        of the cross.
                        See also under 'Lamb'.
                        Isa.53:7;
                        Acts 8:32

               ii.   A METAPHOR for God's people
                        who are meek in nature and who,
                        in total dependency, follow Christ,
                        their heavenly Shepherd.
                        Ps.44:11,22; 49:14; 74:1; 78:52;
                        79:13; 100:3; 119:176;
                        Song.1:7*,8*; Jer.50:6;
                        Ezek.34:6-31; Mic.2:12;
                        Zech.10:2*; 13:7;
                        Matt.10:16; 25:32,33; 26:31;
                        Mk.14:27; Jn.10:1-27; 21:16,17;
                        Rom.8:36; Heb.13:20
                        [*AV translates as 'flock']

               iii.   A SIMILE for those who foolishly
                        go astray from God in search of
                        their own pleasure and who, apart
                        from his grace, are heading for
                        destruction.
                        Isa.53:6; Jer.12:3;
                        Ezek.34:20*,22*;
                        Matt.10:6; 15:24; 18:12,13;
                        Lk.15:4-6; 1 Pet.2:25
                        [*AV translates as 'cattle']

iv.   A SIMILE for those who are
       confused or distressed, or who are
       suffering helplessly under the
       calamities of life.
       2 Sam.24:17; 2 Chr.18:16;
       Isa.13:14; Mic.5:8;
       Matt.9:36; Mk.6:34

Shepherd(s)   i.   A METAPHOR for Christ who
                         guides, protects and cares for his
                         people as a shepherd does for his
                         sheep.
                         NIV only - Gen.48:15; Ps.28:9;
                         Mic.5:4; 7:14
                         Matt.2:6; Rev.7:17
                         AV and NIV - Gen.49:24;
                         Num.27:17; Ps.23:1; 80:1;
                         Ecc.12:11; Isa.40:11; Jer.31:10;
                         Zech.13:7;
                         Matt.25:32; 26:31; Mk.14:27;
                         Jn.10:2-16; Heb.13:20;
                         1 Pet.2:25; 5:4

                  ii.   A METAPHOR for a leader - a
                         king or a teacher or a pastor.
                         NIV only -2 Sam.5:2; 7:7;
                         1 Chr.11:2; 17:6; Ps.78:71,72;
                         Isa.13:14;
                         Acts 20:28; 1 Pet.5:2; Jude 12;
                         AV and NIV - 1 Ki.22:17;
                         Isa.44:28; 56:11; 63:11;
                         Jer.3:15*; 10:21*; 12:10*;
                         17:16*; 22:22*; 23:1-4*;
                         25:34-36; 49:19; 50:6,44;
                         Ezek.34:2-10; Mic.5:5; Nah.3:18;
                         Zech.10:2,3; 11:3-17;
                         Matt.9:36; Mk.6:34
                         [*AV translates as 'pastors']

Shield

A METAPHOR for God's protection of
believers from all that would harm them
in a spiritual and an eternal sense.
See also under 'Cover'
NIV only - Deut.32:10; Ps.7:10;
89:18; Zech.12:8;
AV and NIV - Gen.15:1; Deut.33:29;
2 Sam.22:3,31*,36; Ps.3:3; 5:12;
18:2*,30*,35; 28:7; 33:20; 35:2;
59:11; 84:9,11; 91:4; 115:9-11;
119:114; 144:2; Pro.2:7*; 30:5;
Eph.6:16
[*AV translates as 'buckler']

Shine(s), Shining,
Shone

i.

A SYMBOL for God's grace
towards his people, revealing to
them his love, holiness, power,
truth, etc.
NIV only - Ps.4:6; 94:1; 118:27;
Rev.21:11;
AV and NIV - Num.6:25;
Deut.33:2; Job 22:28; 29:3;
33:30*; Ps.31:16; 50:2; 67:1;
80:1,3,7,19; 119:135; Isa.60:1+;
Matt.17:2; Lk.1:79+; 2:9; 11:36;
Jn.1:5; Acts 12:7; 2 Cor.4:6;
Eph.5:14+; 2 Pet.1:19; 1 Jn.2:8;
Rev.1:16; 21:23
[*AV translates as 'enlightened';
+AV translates as 'give light']

ii.

A SYMBOL for the holy
splendour of the angels and,
especially, for the righteous lives
of true believers.
NIV only - Ps.37:6; Pro.13:9;
Isa.62:1;
AV and NIV - Dan.12:3;
Matt.5:16; 13:43; Acts 10:30*;

Phil.2:15; Rev.15:6+
[*AV translates as 'bright';
+AV translates as 'white linen']

iii. The withdrawal of shining light
SYMBOLIZES the judgment of
God.
See also under 'Darkness'.
NIV only - Lk.23:45;
AV and NIV - Ezek.32:8*;
Joel 2:10; 3:15;
Rev.18:23
[*AV translates as 'bright']

Shock   See under 'Sheaves'.

Shower(s)   A SIMILE and a SYMBOL used to
describe an abundance of blessing from
God on his people, sometimes through
his servants.
See also under 'Rain'.
Deut.32:2; Ps.72:6; Isa.45:8*;
Ezek.22:24+; 34:26; Mic.5:7;
Zech.10:1
[*AV translates as 'pour';
+AV translates as 'rained']

Sickle   A METAPHOR for that which ushers
believers into their eternal reward and the
wicked into judgment. Or, maybe, a
SYMBOL for judgment itself.
Joel 3:13;
Mk.4:29; Rev.14:14-19

Sight   See under 'Eye(s)' and 'Face'.

Signet   See under 'Seal'.

Silver   i.   A METAPHOR for the precious
and enduring quality of a
believer's new nature.

Ps.66:10; Pro.10:20; 25:4,11;
27:21; Song.1:11; 8:9;
Zech.13:9; Mal.3:3;
1 Cor.3:12; 2 Tim.2:20

ii.   A SIMILE and SYMBOL for the precious and enduring quality of Christ and his Word.
Ps.12:6; Pro.2:4; 3:14;
Zech.6:11

Six

The SYMBOLIC number of Man - created on the sixth day. However, the number is also sometimes thought to suggest imperfection or incompleteness, as one less than seven.

The number of the beast - 666 - represents Man in outright rebellion against God - triple 6! That is, Man worshipping himself and attempting to live without God in every way.
Gen.1:26-31; Dan.3:1;
Rev.13:18

**Sleep, Sleeping
Sleeper**

i.   A METAPHOR for a state of spiritual drowsiness and lack of awareness, or even for a state of unbelief.
Isa.56:10;
Mk.13:36; 14:37; Eph.5:14;
1 Thess.5:6

ii.   A METAPHOR for death.
Ps.13:3; 76:5; Jer.51:39,57;
Dan.12:2;
Jn.11:11,13; 1 Cor.11:30

iii.   A METAPHOR for the apparent lack of concern and activity of

God at times when his people need
his help.   In this way God tests
their faith and causes them to pray
more earnestly.
Ps.44:23; 78:65; 121:4;
Matt.8:24; Mk.4:38; 2 Pet.2:3*
[*AV translates as 'slumbereth']

Slips   See under 'Vine(s)'.

Slumber   See under 'Sleep'.

Smoke   i.   A SYMBOL for the holiness and
                         wrath of God against sin.
                         Ex.19:18; 20:18; 2 Sam.22:9;
                         Ps.18:8; 104:32; 144:5; Isa.6:4;
                         9:18; 14:31; 30:27[NIV only];
                         34:10; Joel 2:30;
                         Acts 2:19; Rev.14:11; 15:8;
                         18:9,18; 19:3

                ii.   A SYMBOL for prayer.
                         See under 'Incense'.
                         Lev.16:13*; Song.3:6;
                         Rev.8:4
                         [*AV translates as 'cloud']

                iii.   A SYMBOL for the frailty and
                         shortness of human life apart from
                         God.
                         Ps.37:20; 68:2; 102:3; Isa.51:6;
                         Hos.13:3

                iv.   A SYMBOL for the soul-
                         destroying effect of sin and of hell.
                         Ps.119:83;
                         Rev.9:2,3

                v.   A SIMILE for the nauseating or
                         offensive nature of sin to one who
                         loves holiness.
                         Pro.10:26; Isa.65:5

Sodom

A SYMBOL and SIMILE for the world in its state of rebellion against God with its vile corruption and immorality, and of God's wrath against such. This symbolism is rooted in the Sodom of history, characterized by such rebellion, corruption and immorality and overthrown by the manifest wrath of God (see Gen. 13:13; 19:1-29).
Deut.29:23; 32:32; Isa.1:9; 13:19; Jer.23:14; 49:18; Ezek.16:46-56; Amos 4:11; Zeph.2:9; Matt.10:15; Lk.17:29; Rom.9:29; 2 Pet.2:6; Jude 7; Rev.11:8, etc.

Soil

See under 'Dust'.

Son(s)

i. A METAPHOR used as a title of Christ. As 'Son of God' he shares the nature of God. As 'Son of man' he shares our human nature. Yet he is one Person.
Ps.2:7,12; 8:4; Isa.9:6; Dan.7:13; Matt.3:17; Mk.2:10; Lk.9:35; Jn.1:14[NIV only]; Acts 7:56; Rom.1:3; 1 Cor.15:28; Col.1:13; Heb.1:2; 2 Pet.1:17; 1 Jn.1:7; Rev.1:13; 12:5*; 14:14, etc.
[*AV translates as 'man child']

ii. A METAPHOR for those who truly belong to God by faith from every age.
Gen.6:2; Ex.4:22,23; Deut.1:31; 1 Chr.22:10; Pro.3:12; Hos.11:1; Mal.3:17; Heb.12:5; Rev.21:7

iii. A METAPHOR used to describe a person's character, e.g. 'sons of thunder' or 'sons of perdition'. This was a common Hebrew form of expression.
1 Sam.20:30; Isa.14:12; 57:3; Ezek.2:1; Dan.3:15; Matt.13:38; Mk.3:17; Jn.12:36*; 1 Thess.5:5*
[*AV translates as 'children']

iv. A METAPHOR for a disciple or a follower.
Josh.7:19; 1 Sam.3:16; 4:16; 24:16;
1 Tim.1:2; 2 Tim.2:1; Tit.1:4; Phm.10; 1 Pet.5:13

v. Sometimes used as a METAPHOR for grandsons or even more remote descendants. More exactly, the Hebrew word for 'son' had this range of meaning.
Ex.39:7*; Lev.24:9; Num.1:10*; Ruth 4:17; Job 25:6*; Neh.9:23*; Ps.11:4*; 105:6*; Isa.14:21*; Matt.1:1
[*AV translates as 'children']

Sour   A METAPHOR for the bitter results of sin due to God's curse on it.
Jer.31:29,30; Ezek.18:2; Rev.10:9,10*
[*AV translates as 'bitter']

Sow(s)(ed), Sower   i. A METAPHOR for the spreading of the gospel and those involved in that work.

See also under 'Seed'.
Isa.55:10;
Matt.13:3-37; Mk.4:3-20;
Lk.8:5; Jn.4:36,37

ii. A METAPHOR for a people's motives and actions, i.e. the contribution of their lives, whether good or bad.
Job 4:8; Pro.11:18; 22:8;
Jer.4:3; Hos.8:7; 10:12;
Matt.13:39; Lk.19:21,22;
2 Cor.9:6; Gal.6:7,8;
James 3:18

iii. A METAPHOR for the disposal of the body after death, e.g. by burial.
1 Cor.15:42-44

Spirit(s)   See under 'Wind'.

Spring(s)   i. A SYMBOL for the Holy Spirit as the one who cleanses us from sin and who refreshes our souls.
See also under 'Water'.
Gen.49:22*; Num.21:17;
Deut.33:28; Ps.84:6*; 114:8+;
Song.4:12; Isa.35:7; 41:18;
45:8; 49:10; 58:11; Jer.17:13;
Jn.4:14; Rev.7:17; 21:6
(*AV translates as 'well';
+AV translates as 'fountain')

ii. A METAPHOR for one's speech and its influence, whether good or bad.
Pro.25:26;
James 3:11,12; 2 Pet.2:17*;
[*AV translates as 'wells']

	iii.	A METAPHOR for a source of strength and encouragement. Jer.51:36; Ezek.31:4[NIV only]; Hos.13:15
	iv.	A METAPHOR for marital relations. Pro.5:16
Square		See under 'Foursquare'.
Staff		See under 'Rod'.
Stallions		See under 'Horse(s)'.
Star	i.	A METAPHOR for the Lord Jesus Christ. Num.24:17; 2 Pet.1:19; Rev.2:28; 22:16
	ii.	A METAPHOR for Satan. Isa.14:12; [Lucifer=Day Star] Rev.8:10,11; 9:1
Stars	i.	A SYMBOL for God's people, i.e. for leaders or pastors, or a SIMILE for the numerous characters of God's people. Gen.22:17; 26:4; 37:9; Ex.32:13; Deut.1:10; 10:22; Neh.9:23; Jer.33:22*; Dan.12:3; Phil.2:15+; Heb.11:12; Rev.1:16,20; 2:1; 3:1; 12:1,4 [*AV translates as 'host of heaven'; +AV translates as 'lights']
	ii.	A SYMBOL for angels. Judg.5:20; Job 38:7; Isa.14:13

	iii.	A SYMBOL for false teachers - 'wandering stars'. Jude 13.

Stone(s)   i.   A SYMBOL for Christ, who is both the foundation and 'capstone' or head of the church.
Ps.118:22; Isa.8:14; 28:16;
Dan.2:34,35,45; Zech.3:9;
Matt.21:42,44; Mk.12:10;
Lk.20:17,18; Acts 4:11;
Rom.9:33; 1 Pet.2:4-8; Rev.2:17

ii.   A SYMBOL for the people of God, i.e. those who are being built on the foundation of Christ into a spiritual temple. The removal of contaminated stones in Lev.14:33-57 seems to suggest a figurative picture discipline.
Ex.25:7; 28:9-21; 39:6-14;
Lev.14:40-45; 1 Ki.5:17,18;
6:36; 7:9-12; 18:31;
Ps.102:14; 1 Cor.3:12; 1 Pet.2:5

iii.   A SYMBOLIC way of commemorating some event or some agreement.
Gen.28:18,22; 31:45,46; 35:14;
Deut.27:2-8; Josh.4:3-22; 24:27
1 Sam.7:12

iv.   A SYMBOL for an idol or some other object of false worship.
NIV only - Ex.23 :24; 34:13;
Deut.7:5; 1 Ki.14:23;
2 Chr.14:3; Hos.3:4; Mic.5:13;
Hab.2:19;
AV and NIV - Lev.26:1;
Deut.29:17; 2 Ki.19:18;

Isa.37:19; Jer.2:27; Ezek.20:32
Rev.9:20

v. A SYMBOL used to describe the heart of an unbeliever which is unloving and unresponsive to God.
See also under 'Rock(s)'.
Ezek.11:19; 36:26;
Mk.4:15,16

vi. A SYMBOL used to describe the gifts and grace he bestows on his creatures - even including Lucifer.
Isa.54:11,12; Ezek.28:13;
Rev.21:19

vii. A SYMBOL for various sins committed by God's people which come between them and the Lord.
Isa.62:10; Lam.3:9

viii. The 'fiery stones' of Ezek. 28:14,16 is most likely a METAPHOR for the seraphim, the holy angels standing in the immediate presence of God. Their 'fieriness' suggests their burning zeal for God's honour.
See under 'Fire'.

Storm   See under 'Wind'.

Straw   See under 'Chaff'.

Stream(s)   A METAPHOR for one's source of strength, prosperity and courage. Ultimately this is from God - his common grace for all mankind, but his special grace, or saving grace, for believers only,

i.e. the indwelling Holy Spirit.
See also under 'River', 'Flood'.
Job 6:15; Ps.46:4; Isa.30:25; 34:9;
Isa.35:6; 44:3*,4+; 66:12;
Amos 5:24
[*AV translates as 'floods';
+AV translates as 'water courses']

Stripes	See under 'Wound'.
Stubble	A SIMILE for the wicked whose lives are worthless insofar as God is concerned and will therefore be burned up like stubble. Ex.15:7; Isa.47:14; Joel 2:5; Ob.18; Nah.1:10; Mal.4:1
Sulphur	See under 'Brimstone'.

Sun	i.	A SYMBOL for a person of prime importance, i.e. the head of a family or a ruler of a nation. Gen.37:9
	ii.	A SYMBOL used to describe the qualities of enduring strength and beauty. Judg.5:31; Ps.72:5,17; 89:36; Matt.13:43
	iii.	A SYMBOL for the qualities of righteousness and truth. Ps.37:6[NIV only]; Song.6:10; Rev.12:1
	iv.	A SYMBOL for God, suggesting especially his power, holiness and grace. Ps.84:11; Isa.60:20; Mal.4:2; Matt.17:2; Lk.1:78*;

Rev.1:16; 10:1
[*AV translates as 'dayspring']

v.   The sun being darkened or setting
      early is a frequent SYMBOL for
      impending   judgment   on
      governments and powers of this
      world.
      Isa.13:10; 24:23; Jer.15:9;
      Ezek.32:7; Joel 2:10,31; 3:15;
      Amos 8:9; Mic.3:6
      Matt.24:29; Mk.13:24; Lk.21:25;
      23:45; Acts 2:20; Rev.6:12; 9:2

vi.   In Old Testament times the sun
      was often a SYMBOLIC object of
      false worship.
      Deut.4:19; 17:3; 2 Ki.23:5,11;
      Job 31:26; Jer.8:2; 43:13*;
      Ezek.8:16
      [*AV translates as
      'Bethshemesh']

vii. The scorching effect of the sun's
      rays is used as a METAPHOR for
      the curse to which nature is subject
      since the fall of mankind into sin.
      Ps.121:6; Song.1:6; Isa.49:10;
      James 1:11; Rev.7:16; 8:12; 16:8

viii. A PERSONIFICATION of the
      part of creation where God's
      wisdom and power is most clearly
      seen.
      Ps.148:3

ix.   The writer of Ecclesiastes'
      frequent use of the phrase 'under
      the sun' is a METAPHOR for
      everywhere in the world.
      Eccl.1:3,9,14, etc.

Sunrise	See under 'Light(s)'.

Swine   A SYMBOL used to describe carnally-minded people whose main interest in life is to satisfy their physical appetites. Also, their dirtiness suggests a sinner revelling in his sin.
Lev.11:7*; Deut.14:8*; Pro.11:22*; Matt.7:6*
[*NIV translates as 'pig']
See also 2 Pet.2:22

Sword(s)

i.   A SYMBOL used to represent the instrument of God's chastisement or judgment.
Gen.3:24; Ex.5:3; Lev.26:6; Num.22:23; Deut.32:41; Josh.5:13; 2 Sam.12:10; 1 Chr.21:12-30; 2 Chr.20:9 Job 19:29; Ps.7:12; 45:3; 149:6; Isa.27:1; Jer.9:16; Ezek.6:3; Hos.7:16; Amos 4:10; Nah.2:13; Zeph.2:12; Zech.9:13; Rom.13:4; Rev.1:16; 2:12,16; 19:15,21

ii.   A METAPHOR for the Word of God - the only weapon by which we can overcome sin and the powers of evil.
Eph.6:17; Heb.4:12

iii.   A SYMBOL for the use of violence to achieve certain aims.
Gen.27:40; Ex.18:4; Matt.26:52

iv.   A METAPHOR for violent death and slaughter.
Gen.34:26; Ex.17:13; Num.21:24;

Deut.13:15; Josh.8:24; Judg.1:8;
1 Sam.22:19; Job 1:15; 27:14;
Ps.17:13; 63:10; Isa.2:4;
Jer.2:30; Mic.4:3; Zech.13:7;
Lk.21:24; Acts 12:2; Rev.6:4,8

v.   A METAPHOR for words or
events that bring sorrow or grief or
condemnation.
Job 5:15; Ps.57:4; 59:7; 64:3;
Pro.5:4; 12:18; 25:18; 30:14;
Isa.49:2;
Lk.2:35

vi.   A METAPHOR for hostility
between people on account of the
gospel.
Matt.10:34

Tabernacle   Certain parts of the tabernacle TYPIFY
Christ whilst other parts SYMBOLIZE
his people. Therefore, the tabernacle as a
whole is a TYPE of the union of God and
his people, and the dwelling of God
among his people, which begins in this
life and is perfected in the hereafter.
See also under 'Tent'.
Ex.25:9; Lev.8:10; Num.1:50;
2 Chr.1:5; Ps.27:5;
Acts 7:44; Heb.8:2,5; 9:2-21;
13:10; Rev.15:5, etc.   cf.John 1:14
which may be literally translated 'The
Word became flesh and tabernacled
among us.'

Table(s)   i.   The 'Table of shewbread' is a
SYMBOL for the consecration of
our lives to God.
Ex.25:23-30*; Lev.24:6; Num.4:7;
1 Ki.7:48; 1 Chr.9:32;

2 Chr.13:11;
Heb.9:2, etc.
[*NIV translates as 'bread of the Presence']

ii.   A SYMBOL used to represent God's provision for his people especially for his provision for their eternal welfare in the Lord Jesus Christ.
Ps.23:5; 78:19; Pro.9:2;
Ezek.41:22; 44:16; Mal.1:7,12;
Matt.15:27; Mk.7:28; Lk.22:30;
1 Cor.10:21(a)

iii.   A SYMBOL used to describe idol worship, i.e. a corruption of (ii).
Isa.65:11; Ezek.23:41;
1 Cor.10:21(b)

Tapestry   See under 'Purple'.

Taste(d)   A METAPHOR for experiencing or being acquainted with someone or something.
See also under 'Drink'.
Job 27:2[NIV only]; Ps.34:8; 119:103;
Song.2:3; 4:16*; Ezek.3:3[NIV only];
Matt.16:28; Mk.9:1; Lk.9:27; 14:24;
Jn.8:52; Heb.2:9; 6:4,5; 1 Pet.2:3;
Rev.10:10[NIV only]
[*AV translates as 'eat']

Tempest   See under 'Wind'.

Temple   A SYMBOL for the church, the people of God - of which the Old Testament temple was a TYPE - sometimes the emphasis being on the assembly of believers in a specific place (the local church, e.g.

1 Cor.3:16,17), sometimes pointing to the universal (or heavenly) church of God (e.g. the references in Revelation). This symbolism reminds us, among other things, that the holy God graciously dwells among his people as he dwelt (in a certain sense) in the temple at Jerusalem under the old covenant.

1 Ki.3:1*; 2 Chr.2:1*; Ezra 1:2*; Ps.5:7; Isa.2:2*; Ezek.8:16; Mal.3:1; Matt.12:6; Mk.11:16; Lk.2:37; Acts 2:46; Rom.9:4[NIV only]; 1 Cor.3:16,17; 6:19; 2 Cor.6:16; Eph.2:21; 2 Thess.2:4; Rev.3:12; 7:15; 11:1,19; 14:15,17; 15:5-8; 16:1,17; 21:22, etc.

[*AV translates as 'house (of the Lord)']

Ten

This number is sometimes thought to SYMBOLIZE completeness in a human sense, i.e. ten nations of Canaan (Gen.15:19-21) and the parable of ten virgins (Matt.25:1-13).
Dan.7:7,24;
Rev.12:3; 13:1; 17:3-16

Tent of meeting

See under 'Tabernacle'.

Tent

i.   A METAPHOR for one's dwelling place, one's family or descendants and sometimes including one's possessions.
Job 5:24*; 11:14*; 19:12*; 20:26*; 22:23*; Ps.52:5+; Pro.14:11*
[*AV translates as 'tabernacle'; +AV translates as 'dwelling place']

ii.   A SYMBOL for the universe, in which God has placed the sun, moon and stars.
Ps.19:4*; 104:2+; Isa.40:22
[*AV translates as 'tabernacle';
+AV translates as 'curtain']

iii.   A SYMBOL for the church.
See also under 'Tabernacle'.
Isa.33:20*; 54:2;
Rev.7:15[NIV only].
[*AV translates as 'tabernacle']

iv.   A SYMBOL for the human body which is the dwelling place of the soul.
Job 4:21[NIV only];
18:6*,14*,15*; Isa.38:12;
2 Cor.5:1*,4*; 2 Pet.1:13*
[*AV translates as 'tabernacle']

v.   A SYMBOL for the Jewish nation which was also a TYPE of the church.
See (iii) above.
Jer.10:20*; Lam.2:4*;
Amos 9:11*;
Acts 15:16*
[*AV translates as 'tabernacle']

Thief

A SYMBOL used to describe the way in which Christ will return to this world, suddenly and unexpectedly. Not to steal but rightfully to claim what belongs to him.
Matt.24:43; Lk.12:39; 1 Thess.5:2,4;
2 Pet.3:10; Rev.3:3; 16:15

Thistle(s)

A SYMBOL for that which is useless, worthless and maybe harmful also. Often

used as a picture of sin and its effects in the heart and life of a person.
Gen.3:18; 2 Ki.14:9; 2 Chr.25:18;
Hos.10:8;
Matt.7:16; Heb.6:8*
[*AV translates as 'briers']

Thorn(s)
Thornbush(es)

i. Similar to the meaning given under 'Thistles'.
Gen.3:18; 2 Sam.23:6; Isa.5:6;
7:23-25; 9:18; 10:17; 27:4;
32:13; 33:12; 34:13; Jer.4:3;
12:13; Ezek.28:24; Hos.9:6;
10:8; Nah.1:10;
Matt.13:7,22; Mk.4:7,18;
Lk.8:7,14; Heb.6:8

ii. A SYMBOL for wicked people who are particularly vicious and aggressive.
Num.33:55; Josh.23:13; Judg.2:3;
Judg.9:14*,15*; Song.2:2;
Isa.55:13; Mic.7:4;
Matt.7:16; Lk.6:44
[*AV translates as 'bramble']

iii. A SYMBOL for painful and unpleasant experiences, as a discipline from the Lord on his people.
Pro.15:19; 22:5; 26:9; Ezek.2:6;
Hos.2:6;
2 Cor.12:7

iv. The burning of thorns is sometimes used as a SIMILE for something lasting only a very brief and rapid time.
Ps.58:9; 118:12; Ecc.7:6

Thousand	A number often used as a METAPHOR for a large, indefinite number of people, things or length of time. Deut.1:11; 7:9; 32:30; Josh.23:10; Job 9:3; 33:23; Ps.50:10; 84:10; 90:4; 91:7; Ecc.6:6; 7:28; Song.4:4; 8:11,12; Isa.30:17; 60:22; 2 Pet.3:8; Rev.20:2-7
Ten thousand	This number is also used as a METAPHOR for a very large number, whilst ten thousand times ten thousand represents a number that is inconceivably vast and countless. Lev.26:8; Deut.32:30; 33:17; 1 Sam.18:7,8; Ps.3:6; 91:7; Song.5:10; Dan.7:10; Mic.6:7; Matt.18:24; 1 Cor.4:15; 14:19; Rev.5:11
One hundred and forty-four thousand.	See under 'Twelve'.
Three	A number often used to represent fulness or completeness, especially with reference to God. Sometimes used with reference to a period of divine judgment. Ex.23:14; Deut.16:16; 2 Sam.24:12,13; 1 Chr.21:10,12; Dan.6:10,13; Amos.1:3-13; 2:1-6; Jon.1:17; Matt.12:40; Mk.9:31; 10:34; Lk.4:25; Acts 10:16; 11:10; James 5:17; Rev.9:18; 16:19; 21:13.
Three and a half, or Time, times and half a time	A SYMBOL for any limited period of time during which evil is allowed to oppress God's people. It can be expressed as 42 months, i.e. $3\frac{1}{2}$ years (Rev.11:2), or 1260 days (Rev.11:3). The background to the

symbolism is the period of Jewish suffering under the Syrian despot Antiochus Epiphanes in 167-164BC (prophesied in Daniel). The various uses of the symbolism in Revelation point to a period of end-age witness, divine protection and pagan antagonism, and are probably a way of referring to the gospel age as a whole. It may be noted that the terrible drought in Israel during Ahab's reign lasted 3½ years (1 Ki.17 and 18). This terrible failure of rains undoubtedly made a great impression on the Jewish national mind, so that 'a time, times and half a time' became proverbial as an expression of a time of severe hardship.
Dan.7:25; 12:7;
Rev.11:2,3,9,11; 12:14

Thresh(ing)

A SYMBOL used to describe a severe judgment or a crushing defeat.
NIV only - Pro.20:26; Hos.13:3;
Mic.4:12;
Matt.3:12; Lk.3:17;
AV and NIV - 2 Ki.13:7;
Isa.21:10; 27:12*; 41:15;
Jer.51:33; Dan.2:35; Amos 1:3;
Mic.4:13; Hab.3:12
[*AV translates as 'beat oft']

Throne(s)

A SYMBOL used to represent sovereignty and authority. Frequently used to symbolize the absolute sovereignty of God over the entire universe.
Gen.41:40; Ex.17:16(NIV only);
Deut.17:18; 1 Sam.2:8; 2 Sam.3:10;
1 Ki.1:13; 2 Ki.15:12; 1 Chr.17:12;
2 Chr.6:10; Ps.11:4; Pro.16:12;

| | Isa.6:1; Jer.14:21; Lam.5:19; Ezek.1:26; Dan.7:9; Zech.6:13; Matt.19:28; Lk.1:32; Acts 2:30; Col.1:16; Heb.1:8; Rev.1:4; 4:2-10; 5:1-13; 22:1,3, etc. |

Thunder   Often used as a SYMBOL for the awesome power of God, sometimes as seen in his mighty angels also.
AV and NIV - Ex.9:23; 20:18;
1 Sam.2:10; Job 26:14; 37:4; 40:9;
Ps.18:13; 29:3; 77:18; 81:7; 104:7;
Isa.29:6;
Jn.12:29; Rev.4:5; 6:1; 8:5; 10:3,4;
11:19; 14:2; 16:18; 19:6;
NIV only - Ps.68:33; Jer.10:13;
51:16; Joel 2:11; 3:16; Amos 1:2

Torch   See under 'Furnace'.

Torrents   See under 'Flood'.

Tower(s)

i. A METAPHOR for God, who provides strong protection and security for those who seek their refuge in him.
2 Sam.22:3*; Ps.18:2*; 61:3;
144:2*; Pro.18:10
[*NIV translates as 'stronghold']

ii. A METAPHOR for the strength and beauty of God's people, the church.
Ps.48:12; Song.4:4; 7:4; 8:10;
Isa.5:2; Mic.4:8

iii. A SYMBOL for people's rebelliousness against God in their seeking protection and security in things other than in him.
Gen.11:4,5; Isa.2:15; 30:25;

Isa.33:18;
Ezek.26:4,9; 27:11; Zeph.3:6*
[*NIV translates as 'stronghold']

iv.   A METAPHOR for the place of
       prophetic vision.
       See also under 'Watchman'.
       Hab.2:1*
       [*NIV translates as 'ramparts']

Traps   See under 'Pit(s)'.

Tread out the corn   See under 'Thresh(ing)'.

Tree(s)   i.   A SYMBOL for the strength and
                          the abundant life of one who
                          firmly trusts in the Lord.
                          Ps.1:3; 37:35; 52:8; 92:12;
                          Song.4:14; 7:8; Isa.44:4*;
                          65:22; Jer.11:19; 17:8;
                          Ezek.47:7,12
                          [*AV translates as 'willows']

                    ii.   A METAPHOR for either the life
                          of an individual person or for a
                          nation. Like a tree they may either
                          flourish under God's blessing or
                          suffer judgment and be stripped
                          bare or uprooted. A barren tree is
                          often used as a SYMBOL for those
                          who have no faith in or love for
                          Christ.
                          Job 19:10; 24:20; Song.2:3;
                          Isa.7:2; 10:19,33*; 14:8; 56:3;
                          Ezek.17:24; 20:47; 31:4-18;
                          Dan.4:10-26; Zech.11:2;
                          Matt.3:10; 7:17-19; 12:33;
                          21:19; Lk.3:9; 6:43,44; Jude 12
                          [*AV translates as 'high ones']

iii. A SYMBOL for the kingdom of God.
Zech.1:8-11;
Matt.13:32; Lk.13:19

iv. A PERSONIFICATION of God's creation which reflects something of God's wisdom, power and love and thus is said to offer him praise.
Ps.96:12; Isa.44:23; 55:12

v. A METAPHOR for the cross. Execution by being hung from a tree represented being under God's curse. Thus Christ suffered the curse of our sin when he died on the cross. See also under particular trees, e.g. fig, olive, palm, etc.
Deut.21:22,23;
Acts 5:30; 10:39; 13:29;
Gal.3:13; 1 Pet.2:24

Tree of knowledge A SYMBOL for that which is forbidden by the laws of God.
Gen.2:9,17; 3:3-17

Tree of life i. A SYMBOL for God's gift of eternal life, the way to which was lost due to mankind's fall into sin, but which is restored to us through the Lord Jesus Christ.
Gen.2:9; 3:22,24;
Rev.2:7; 22:2,14,19*
[*AV translates as 'book of life']

ii. A METAPHOR for that which is good and beneficial and which brings joy and gladness.
Pro.11:30; 13:12; 15:4

Troops		See under 'Horse(s)'.
Troublemakers		See under 'Belial'.
Trumpet(s)	i.	Used to indicate the importance of an announcement or an event. Lev.23:24: Josh.6:16; Judg.3:27; 1 Sam.13:3; 2 Sam.2:28; 1 Ki.1:34; 2 Ki.9:13; Neh.4:20; Job 39:24; Jer.4:5
	ii.	A SYMBOL for the calling of attention to some announcement or event. Often associated with God's judgments. NIV only - Rev.9:1,13; 10:7; 11:15; AV and NIV - Ex.19:16; Isa.27:13; Ezek.33:4-6; Hos.5:8; Joel 2:1,15; Amos 2:2; Zech.9:14 Matt.24:31; 1 Cor.14:8; 15:52; 1 Thess.4:16; Heb.12:19; Rev.1:10; 4:1; 8:2-13; 9:14
Twelve		The number of the sons of Israel and afterwards used to SYMBOLIZE the entire people of God. Gen.17:20; Ex.24:4; Lev.24:5; Num.7:84; Deut.1:23; Josh.4:8; 1 Ki.18:31; Ezra 8:35; Matt.10:1-5; 19:29; Mk.3:14; Lk.6:13; Jn.6:67; Acts 26:7; James 1:1; Rev.7:5-8; 12:1; 21:12,14,20,21; 22:2, etc.
Twelve times twelve		SYMBOLIZES the people of God in both Old and New Testament times. When multiplied by 1000, to give 144,000, this represents the total number

of God's elect in every age, being a vast number.
See also under 'Thousand'.
Rev.7:4; 14:1,3

Tyre

The king of Tyre may be used as a SYMBOL for Satan who was similarly a powerful and majestic ruler who brought terrible judgment on himself because of his pride and rebellion against God.
Ezek.28:11-19*
[*AV translates as 'Tyrus']

Unclean

A SYMBOL used to represent the pollution and defilement of spirit caused by sin.
Gen.7:2*; Lev.5:2; Num.5:2+;
Deut.12:15; Judg.13:4; 1 Sam.20:26*;
2 Chr.29:16; Ezra 2:62**; Neh.7:65**;
Ecc.9:2; Isa.6:5; Lam.1:8[NIV only];
Ezek.4:14**; Hos.9:3;
Matt.15:11+; Mk.7:2+; Acts 10:14;
Rom.14:14; 1 Cor.7:14; 2 Cor.6:17;
Heb.9:13; Rev.18:2, etc.
[*AV translates as 'not clean';
+AV translates as 'defiled';
**AV translates as 'polluted']

Unleavened

A SYMBOL used to describe holiness, i.e. those who have kept themselves free from the influence of wrong teachings and bad examples. The passover was also called the Feast of Unleavened Bread. In this case the unleavened bread represents the sinless humanity of Christ.
See also under 'Bread' and 'Leaven'.
Ex.12:20; 13:7; Deut.16:3-16;
1 Cor.5:7,8 [AV only]

Untempered morter   See under 'Wall iv (whitewashed)'.

Valley(s)   i.   A valley is a depression in the land
                             surface and is often in the shade, so
                             it is often used as a SYMBOL for
                             the place of trial or testing of
                             God's people but where also they
                             often experience God's special
                             help and blessing.
                             Ps.23:4; 84:6; Song.2:1;
                             Isa.41:18; Ezek.37:1,2; Hos.2:15;

                     ii.   Because a valley forms a natural
                             barrier it is sometimes used as a
                             SYMBOL for our sins which
                             separate us from God.
                             Isa.40:4;
                             Lk.3:5

                     iii.   Valleys are often very fertile, so
                             they are used as a SYMBOL to
                             describe the abundance of God's
                             blessings which he lavishes on his
                             people.
                             Num.24:6; Deut.8:7; 11:11;
                             Ps.65:13; Song.6:11; Isa.65:10;
                             Joel 3:18

                     iv.   A SYMBOL for the place where
                             terrible sins are committed, and
                             thus the place of God's judgment.
                             The valley of Ben Hinnom outside
                             Jerusalem was where child
                             sacrifices were committed and
                             where rubbish continually burned.
                             Thus, it became a clear picture of
                             hell (from the Greek name
                             'Gehenna').
                             Isa.22:1,5; 28:1,4; Jer.2:23;
                             7:31,32; 19:2,6; 21:13; 31:40;

32:35; Ezek.39:11,15; Hos.1:5;
Joel 3:2,12,14; Amos 1:5*
[*AV translates as 'plain']

v.   A valley can form a natural way
through a mountain range. Thus, it
is used as a SYMBOL for God's
way of deliverance of his people
from judgment, i.e. through
Christ.
Zech.14:4,5

vi.   The expression 'mountains and
valleys' and similar ones are used
as SYNECDOCHES for the entire
land referred to in the context.
Ezek.6:3; 31:12; 32:5; 36:4,6;
Mic.1:4

Veil(ed) Vail

i.   A SYMBOL for that which
prevents people from perceiving
and understanding the truth of
Christ. This may either refer to
one's unbelief or to the Lord not
revealing this truth, or both.
Ex.26:31*; 34:33-35; 36:35*;
40:3*; Lev.16:2*,15*; 21:23*;
24:3*;
Matt.27:51*; Mk.15:38*;
Lk.23:45*; 2 Cor.3:13-16; 4:3+;
Heb.6:19*; 9:3*
[*NIV translates as 'curtain';
+AV translates as 'hid']

ii.   A METAPHOR for death.
Isa.25:7*
[*NIV translates as 'sheet']

iii.   A METAPHOR for the physical
human body of Christ which had

to be broken for God's way of salvation to be revealed (compare i.) Heb.10:20 [NIV 'curtain']

iv.   A SYMBOL for the way people try and hide the shame of their sinfulness.
NIV only - Song.1:7; 4:1,3; Isa.47:2

Venom   See under 'Gall' and 'Poison'.

Vexation of spirit   See under 'Wind'.

Vine(s)

i.   A SYMBOL used to represent fruitfulness and prosperity in either a physical or a spiritual sense. Conversely, the blighting or withering of the vine symbolizes judgment.
Gen.40:9,10; 49:11;
Judg.9:12,13; 1 Ki.4:25;
2 Ki.18:31; Job 15:33; Ps.78:47;
128:3; Song.2:13; 6:11; 7:8,12;
Isa.7:23; 16:8,9; 24:7; 32:12;
36:16; Jer.5:17; 8:13; 48:32;
Hos.2:12; Joel 1:11,12; 2:22;
Mic.4:4; Nah.2:2; Hab.3:17;
Hag.2:19; Zech.3:10; Mal.3:11

ii.   A SYMBOL for Christ who is the one who gives support (or upholds) and nourishment to his people in a spiritual sense. (N.B. Joseph is a type of Christ).
Gen.49:22*;
Jn.15:1-5
[*AV translates as 'bough']

iii. A SYMBOL for the people of God, either Israel B.C. or the church A.D.
Ps.80:8-16; Isa.5:2; Jer.2:21a; Ezek.15:2,6; 17:6-8; Hos.10:1; 14:7; Joel 1:7

iv. A SYMBOL for original sin which is the source of all the wickedness and rebelliousness in people's hearts.
Deut.32:32; Isa.17:10*; Jer.2:21b; Rev.14:18
[*AV translates as 'strange slips']

Viper   A SYMBOL for the wicked who, like vipers, are sly and vicious by nature.
Job 20:16; [NIV 'adder']
Matt.3:7; 12:34; 23:33; Lk.3:7

Virgin(s)   i. SYMBOLICALLY used to describe those who have not yielded themselves to idolatry but who have kept themselves faithful to the LORD or Christ. This is an appropriate symbol because, in Old Testament times, much idol worship involved sexual misconduct. Also, the idea of 'covenant' implies the relationship of love and loyalty between God and the virgin bride he has betrothed to himself.
2 Ki.19:21; Isa.37:22; Jer.14:17; 31:4,21;
Matt.25:1-10; 2 Cor.11:2
[See also Rev.14:4]

| | ii. | A SYMBOL for the most tender and innocent section of a nation. If they are guilty and ready for judgment then that nation as a whole must be very guilty indeed. Isa.23:12; 47:1; Jer.18:13; 46:11; Lam.1:15; 2:13; Ezek.23:3,8; Amos 5:2 |

Vulture   See under 'Eagle'.

| **Walk(s)(ed)(ing)** | i. | When applied to God it is a METAPHOR for God being actively present amongst his people, in fellowship with them in the way he originally intended. Gen.3:8; Lev.26:12; 2 Cor.6:16; Rev.2:1 |
| | ii. | A METAPHOR for one's habitual way of life or to one's experiences along life's way. People generally either 'walk' in humble obedience to God or in sin and disobedience. AV only - Eph.4:1,17; 5:2, etc. NIV only- Pro.8:20*; Hos.11:3+; Mic.2:3+; AV and NIV - Gen.5:22; 17:1; Deut.5:33; 10:12; 11:22; 19:9; 26:17; 28:9; 30:16; Josh.22:5; Judg.2:22; 1 Sam.8:3,5; 1 Ki.2:3,4; 2 Ki.21:22; 2 Chr.6:16; Neh.5:9; Job 31:5; Ps.1:1; 26:3; Pro.2:7; Ecc.2:14; Isa.2:3; Jer.6:16; Dan.4:37; Amos 3:3; Zech.3:7; Jn.8:12; Rom.4:12; Col.3:7; 1 Jn.1:6,7; 2:6,11; 2 Jn.4,6; 3 Jn.3,4; Rev.21:24 [*AV translates as 'lead'; +AV translates as 'go'] |

iii. To walk on someone is a METAPHOR for humiliating them.
See also under 'Way(s)'.
Ezek.36:12

Wall(s)(ed)

i. A SYMBOL used to represent some great difficulty or threat or something that restricts.
See also under 'Hedge'.
Gen.49:22; 2 Sam.22:30;
Ps.18:29; Lam.3:7*; Ezek.4:3;
Hos.2:6;
Eph.2:14
[*AV translates as 'hedged']

ii. A SYMBOL for the strong protection and security believers have in God.
1 Sam.25:16; Ps.51:18; 122:7;
Song.2:9; 5:7; 8:9,10; Isa.25:4;
26:1; 49:16; 56:5; 60:10,18;
62:6; Jer.1:18; 15:20;
Ezek.40:5; 41:5,6; Mic.7:11;
Zech.2:5;
Matt.21:33*; Mk.12:1*;
Rev.21:12-18
[*AV translates as 'hedge(d)']

iii. A SYMBOL for the things of this life in which people seek their security, but which cannot provide lasting safety, e.g. wealth, human wisdom, strength, etc.
Ps.62:3; 80:12*; Pro.18:11;
Isa.5:5; 22:12; 30:13;
Ezek.13:5*,10-15; 22:30*;
38:11,20; Joel 2:9;
Amos 4:3[NIV only]; 5:19;
Zech.2:4
[*AV translates as 'hedge(s)']

iv. A whitewashed wall is a METAPHOR for a false prophet or a hypocrite.
Ezek.13:10-15*;
Acts 23:3
[*AV translates as 'untempered morter']

v. The vertical wall in Amos' vision is a SYMBOL for God's perfect righteousness which he requires of his people.
See also under 'Plumbline'.
Amos 7:7

vi. A SYMBOL for self-discipline by which unruly passions are held in check.
Pro.25:28

Wash(es)(ed)(ing)   A SYMBOL used to describe the cleansing of our souls from sin through the blood of Christ. The ceremonial washings of the Old Testament typified this and baptism symbolizes it. Some say that washing all over symbolizes our justification whilst the washing of hands or feet symbolizes the daily forgiveness of sins that a believer needs.
Gen.49:11; Ex.19:10; Lev.11:25;
Num.8:7; Deut.21:6; 2 Ki.5:10;
Job 9:30; Ps.26:6; 51:2; Song.5:3;
Isa.1:16; Jer.4:14; Ezek.16:4;
Matt.15:2; Mk.7:4; Lk.11:38;
Jn.13:5; Acts 22:16; 1 Cor. 6:11;
Eph.5:26; Tit.3:5; Jas.4:8*;
Rev.7:14; 22:14[NIV only], etc.
[*AV translates as 'cleanse']

Watchman(men)

A SYMBOL for leaders of God's people such as pastors or elders, who are to be constantly watching over the souls of their congregations and to warn them of spiritual dangers and temptations.
Song.3:3; 5:7; Isa.21:11,12; 52:8; 56:10; 62:6; Jer.6:17; 31:6; Ezek.3:17; 33:2,6,7

Water(s)(ed)

i. A SYMBOL for various kinds of trials or for judgments. These may be means whereby God punishes the wicked but from which he delivers his people, even though they may have to experience them a while.
2 Sam.5:20; 22:17; Job 22:11; Ps.18:16; 66:12; 69:1,2,14; 144:7; Isa.28:17; Jer.8:14; 9:15; 23:15; Lam.3:54; Ezek.26:19; Hos.5:10; Rev.12:15

ii. A SYMBOL for the Holy Spirit through whom God gives blessing and refreshment and strength. Either for the common grace given to all people or for the special grace reserved for God's elect.
Num.20:8,10,11; Deut.8:15; Job 29:19; Ps.1:3; 42:1; 78:20; 105:41; 114:8; Song.4:15; 5:12; Isa.1:30; 12:3; 27:3; 30:25; 32:2; 33:16; 35:6; 41:17,18; 43:20; 48:21; 49:10; Jer.2:13; 17:8,13; 31:9; Ezek.16:4,9; 17:5,7,8; 32:2; 34:18; 36:25; 47:1-12; Hos.6:3*; Joel 3:18; Nah.2:8; Zech.14:8;

Jn.4:10-15; 7:38; 1 Cor.3:7,8;
Eph.5:26; Heb.9:19; 10:22;
2 Pet.2:17; Rev.7:17; 21:6;
22:1,17
[*AV translates as 'former rain']

iii.   A SYMBOL for something that is
either soaked up or which gushes
forth, e.g. the groans of an
oppressed people are said to pour
out like water, whereas the wicked
are said to drink wickedness like
water.
Job 3:24; 15:16; 34:7; Ps.79:3;
109:18; Jer.9:1,18; Lam.2:19;
Mic.1:4

iv.   Water erosion or water flowing
away, etc. are used as SIMILES
for the decay of one's strength and
vigour with age and with the
various trials of life.
Job 14:19; Ps.22:14; 58:7

v.   A SYMBOL for sexual inter-
course.
Pro.5:15,16; 9:17;
Jn.3:5 (according to one view of
this controversial verse).

vi.   A SYMBOL for gracious words
which give joy and gladness to the
hearer.
Pro.25:25; Jas.3:11,12 (the fresh
water only).

vii.   A SYMBOL for human help and
support which will all fail in the
day of God's judgment.
Isa.8:7; Jer.2:18; 48:34;
Ezek.7:17

viii.   (a)   A SYMBOL for wickedness.
Jer.6:7

      (b)   A METAPHOR for sinful speech.
Jas.3:11

ix.   The water of baptism SYMBOLIZES the cleansing of our souls from sin, i.e. justification and sanctification.
See also under 'Baptism' and 'Washing'.
N.B. In Jesus' baptism he was not testifying to his repentance but, as our representative, he was living in full obedience to his Father on our behalf.
Matt.3:11; Mk.1:8; Lk.3:16; Jn.1:26,31,33; Acts 1:5;11:16; 1 Pet.3:20,21[NIV only]; 1 Jn.5:6,8

x.   The waters of the River Euphrates are a METAPHOR for God's restraint of those who seek to destroy the church.
Rev.16:12

xi.   A METAPHOR for the nations and peoples of the world as they are under the power of Satan and in opposition to God.
See also under 'Sea'.
Rev.17:1,15

xii.   A SIMILE for the flow of life's history, as events come and go like the flowing waters in a river.
Job 11:16

xiii.   Deep waters are used as a METAPHOR for the deep and hidden thoughts within a person's heart (or subconscious).
Pro.18:4; 20:5

xiv.   'As waters cover the sea' is a SIMILE for the universality of the true knowledge of God among people living in the new earth.
Isa.11:9; Hab.2:14

xv.   The roaring of rushing waters is a SIMILE for the fury of ungodly nations.
Isa.17:12,13; Jer.46:7,8; 51:55

xvi.   The roaring of rushing waters is also used as a SIMILE of the voice of the Lord sounding forth in great power.
Ezek.1:24; 43:2;
Rev.1:15

xvii.   Again, the roaring of rushing water is a SIMILE for the sound of the great choir of the redeemed in heaven.
Rev.14:2; 19:6

Water courses,   See under 'Streams'.

Wave(s)   i.   As waves batter against the shore, they are used as a SYMBOL for repeated or continuous afflictions.
Ps.42:7; 88:7; Jer.51:42,55;
Ezek.26:3

ii.   A SYMBOL for abundance as the vast number of waves on the surface of the sea.
Isa.48:18

iii.	A METAPHOR for those who oppress and persecute the Lord's people. Zech.10:11 [NIV 'surging sea']
iv.	A SIMILE for a doubting professing believer who cannot make up his mind who or what to believe. Jas.1:6
v.	A SIMILE for false teachers who are motivated by their lusts just as waves are driven by the wind. Jude 13.

Way(s)

i.   A METAPHOR for a person's character or general behaviour, whether it be good or bad, obedient or disobedient, believing or unbelieving, etc.
See also under 'Walk'.
Gen.6:12; Ex.33:13; Num.22:32;
Deut.5:33; Josh.1:8; Judg.2:19;
1 Sam.12:33; 2 Sam.22:31;
2 Ki.8:27; 2 Chron.27:6;
Job 34:21; Ps.1:6; Pro.2:8;
Isa.26:7; Jer.6:16; Lam.3:40;
Ezek.3:18; Dan.5:23; Hos.4:9;
Amos 2:7; Mic.4:2; Hag.1:5;
Zech.1:6;
Matt.7:13; Mk.12:13; Lk.1:79;
Jn.10:1; Acts 18:26; Rom.11:33;
1 Cor.12:31; Jas.1:8; 2 Pet.2:2;
Jude 11; Rev.15:3, etc.

ii.   A METAPHOR for Christ, for it is through him alone that we can come before God and find peace and acceptance with him.
Jn.14:6; Heb.9:8; 10:20

	iii.	The 'way of all the earth' is a METAPHOR for bodily death. Josh.23:14; 1 Ki.2:2

Weapon   See under 'Armour'.

Wedding   See under 'Marriage'.

Week(s)   These are SYMBOLIC periods of time of indefinite length (i.e. unknown to anyone except God), during which God is working out his redemptive purposes. See also under 'Seven(th)'. Dan.9:24-27 [AV only]

Well(s)   i.   A METAPHOR for the means of grace, i.e. the prophets' teaching, the Levitical rituals. These in turn were TYPICAL of the means of grace in the New Testament church: preaching, sacraments, etc. Isa.12:3

                 ii.   Waterless wells is a METAPHOR for false prophets or teachers. They appear to be true on the surface but their ministry is barren and useless. 2 Pet.2:17* N.B. A similar picture of the false prophets as waterless clouds is given in Jude 12. [*NIV translates as 'springs']

Wheat   i.   A SYMBOL for the abundance of God's provision for his people, especially as a picture of their spiritual nourishment, i.e. the Word of God. Ps.81:16; 147:14; Song.7:2; Jer.23:28; 31:12; Joel 2:24

ii.   A SYMBOL for one's stock of provisions of the everyday necessities of life.
Jer.12:13;
Rev.6:6

iii.   A SYMBOL for true believers. In the day of judgment they will carefully be separated from the ungodly as wheat is from chaff during harvest.
See also under 'Chaff' and 'Harvest'.
Matt.3:12; 13:25-30; Lk.3:17; 22:31

iv.   A SYMBOL for the Lord Jesus Christ. His death was like the planting of a wheat seed which resulted in a great harvest of people redeemed to God.
Jn.12:24

Wheel(s)   A SYMBOL for great mobility and speed. Applied to God's throne and to the cherubim. This shows us that God's dominion and power extends to all places instantaneously.
Ezek.1:15-21; 3:13; 10:2-19; 11:22

Whirlwind   A SYMBOL for God's great power extending from heaven to earth. Often used as a picture of his wrath on unrepentant sinners.
See also under 'Wind'.
2 Ki.2:1,11; Ps.77:18[NIV only];
Pro.1:27; Isa.5:28; 21:1; 40:24;
66:15; Jer.4:13; 23:19;
Hos.4:19[NIV only]; 8:7; Nah.1:3;
Zech.7:14

White	A colour used to SYMBOLIZE holiness and righteousness and perhaps, sometimes, victory. Applied to God, to angels and to the redeemed. Gen.49:12; Ps.51:7; Isa.1:18; Dan.7:9 Matt.17:2; 28:3; Mk.9:3; 16:5; Jn.20:12; Acts 1:10; Rev.1:14; 2:17; 3:4,5,18; 4:4; 6:2,11; 7:9,13,14; 14:14; 19:11,14; 20:11
White linen	See under 'Shine(s)'.
Whitewashed	A METAPHOR for falsity or hypocrisy. Ezek.13:10-15*; 22:28*; Matt.23:27+; Acts 23:3+ [*AV translates as 'untempered morter'; +AV translates as 'whited']
Whore	See under 'Harlot'.
Wicked men	See under 'Belial'.
Wife	A SYMBOL for the people of God. Sometimes used for all who outwardly profess to belong to God, even though most may be false (as in Ezek.16). At other times referring to those who are the genuine church of God. See also under 'Bride'. Isa.54:6; Ezek.16:32; Rev.21:9
Willows	See under 'Tree(s)'.
Wind(s) Windstorm	i. A SYMBOL used to describe God's great power and speed of action. 2 Sam.22:11; Ps.18:10; 104:3

ii.   A SYMBOL for a thorough defeat
       or destruction, often as a judgment
       from God. Especially 'east wind'
       or 'scorching wind' which blows
       in from the hot desert.
       Job 27:21; 30:22; 37:21; Ps.1:4;
       11:6*; 18:42; 35:5; 48:7;
       68:2[NIV only]; 83:13; 103:16;
       Isa.11:15; 17:13; 24:20 (NIV
       only); 27:8; 28:2+; 41:16;
       57:13; 64:6; Jer.4:11,12; 13:24;
       18:17; 22:22; 30:23**;
       Ezek.5:2; 13:13; 17:10; 19:12;
       27:26; Dan.2:35; Hos.13:15;
       Jon.4:8;
       Matt.7:25,27; Rev.6:13; 7:1
       [*AV translates as 'tempest';
       +AV translates as 'storm';
       **AV translates as 'whirlwind']

iii.   A SYMBOL for that which is vain,
       empty, useless, nothing,
       meaningless, etc. Used for such
       things as boastful speech, idolatry,
       the pleasures of sin, etc.
       Job 6:26; 8:2; 15:2; Pro.11:29;
       Ecc.1:14*,17*; 2:11*,17*,26*;
       4:4*,6*,16*; 5:16; 6:9*;
       Isa.26:18; 41:29; Jer.2:24; 5:13
       Hos.8:7; 12:1;
       Matt.11:7; Lk.7:24; Eph.4:14;
       Jas.1:6; Jude 12
       [*AV translates as 'vexation of
       spirit']

iv.   A SYMBOL for a relentless or
       pursuing adversary.
       Job 30:15; Pro.27:16; Isa.32:2;
       Hab.1:9,11[NIV only]

v.   A SYMBOL for that which is
     beyond the power of people to
     control or to understand.
     Pro.30:4; Ecc.8:8*; 11:4,5*;
     Amos 4:13
     [*AV translates as 'spirit']

vi. A SYMBOL for the Holy Spirit.
     Jn.3:8; Acts 2:2

vii. A SYMBOL used to describe the
     swiftness with which the angels
     respond to God's commands.
     Zech.5:9;
     Heb.1:7*
     [*AV translates as 'spirits']

viii. The 'four winds' is used as a
      METAPHOR for either every
      direction or everywhere.
      Jer.49:36; Ezek.37:9; Dan.7:2;
      8:8; 11:4; Zech.2:6;
      Matt.24:31; Rev.7:1

Wine   i.   A SYMBOL for the wrath of God
              which causes people to stagger
              and reel, not from intoxication but
              from terror.
              See also under 'Drink'.
              Ps.60:3; 75:8; Isa.49:26; 51:21;
              Jer.13:12; 23:9; 25:15; 51:7;
              Rev.14:8,10; 16:19

         ii. A SYMBOL for false worship and
              teaching or idolatry.
              Isa.65:11*;
              Rev.17:2; 18:3
              [*AV translates as 'drink offer-
              ing']

iii. A SYMBOL for the grace of God or the gospel and its provisions. In the Gospels, it is 'new wine'.
Gen.49:11,12; Pro.9:5; Song.5:1; 7:2*,9; 8:2; Isa.25:6; 55:1; Hos.14:7; Zech.9:15; Matt.9:17; Mk.2:22; Lk.5:37; [*AV translates as 'liquor']

iv. The 'wine of violence' is a METAPHOR for violence as a habit or a way of life.
Pro.4:17

v. Being like 'bottled-up wine' is a SIMILE for having a strongly repressed desire - in this case, to speak.
Job 32:19

vi. A SYMBOL for temporal blessings or luxuries or 'the good life'. These may refer to those things unbelievers value so highly or, in some cases, they may be taken as TYPES of gospel age blessings.
See under (ii) and (iii).
Gen.27:28; Num.18:12; Deut.7:13; 2 Ki.18:32; 2 Chr.31:5; Neh.10:37; Ps.4:7; 104:15; Pro.3:10; 21:17; Ecc.9:7; Song.1:2,4; 4:10; Isa.1:22; Jer.31:12; Lam.2:12; Ezek.27:18; Hos.2:8; Joel 2:24; 3:18; Amos 9:13,14; Mic.2:11; Zech.9:17; Rev.6:6; 18:13

vii.   Wine left settling on its dregs is a SIMILE for those who are complacent and presumptuous, going on in their selfishness without alertness to God, his judgment against sin and the availability of his grace.
Zeph.1:12[NIV only]

Winepress(es)

A SYMBOL for God's judgment, i.e. the place where his enemies are crushed.
Isa.63:2*; Lam.1:15;
Rev.14:19,20; 19:15
[*AV translates as 'winefat']

Wineskin(s)

i.   A 'wineskin in the smoke' is a SIMILE for a believer suffering the scorn and mockery of the ungodly.
Ps.119:83*
[*AV translates as 'bottle in the smoke']

ii.   A METAPHOR for a 'religious' framework. Thus old and new wineskins represent, respectively, old Judaism with its religious observances and (perhaps) changed lives (closely related to but not identical with the old and new covenants.)
Matt.9:17*; Mk.2:22*; Lk.5:37*
[*AV translates as 'old bottles']

Wing(s)

i.   A METONYMY for speed and mobility. Often used with reference both to God and to his angels.
Ex.25:20; 37:9; 2 Sam.22:11;
1 Ki.6:24; 2 Chr.3:11;
Ps.18:10; 104:3; Isa.6:2;
Ezek.1:6,11; Zech.5:9;
Rev.4:8, etc.

ii.   A SYMBOL for the loving care and protection the Lord gives to those who come to him.
Ex.19:4; Deut.32:11; Ruth 2:12; Ps.17:8; 36:7; 57:1; 61:4; 63:7; 91:4; Mal.4:2; Matt.23:37; Lk.13:34; Rev.12:14

iii.   A METAPHOR for something that soon disappears, in this case earthly riches.
Pro.23:5

iv.   A METAPHOR for something beautiful and graceful.
Ps.68:13

v.   A METAPHOR for the means of making a rapid escape from an unpleasant situation.
Ps.55:6; 139:9

vi.   A SYMBOL for the speedy conquest of an invading army.
Isa.8:8; Jer.48:40; 49:22; Ezek.17:3,7; Dan.7:4,6

vii.   A METAPHOR for the rapid spread of demonic powers (i.e. fallen angels) throughout the world.
Rev.9:9

viii. A SIMILE for the grace God gives his people enabling them to remain faithful to him where even the greatest natural strength fails.
Isa.40:31

Winnow(s)(ing)   A SYMBOL for the separation of good
                                 from evil for the purpose of judgment,
                                 based on the practice of tossing the
                                 threshed wheat (for example) lying on
                                 the threshing-floor, into the air, using a
                                 winnowing fork.   This allowed the
                                 prevailing wind to separate the light-
                                 weight chaff from the authentic grain.
                                 See also under 'Threshing'.
                                 Pro.20:8,26*; Isa.41:16+; Jer.4:11+;
                                 15:7+; 51:2+;
                                 Matt.3:12+; Lk.3:17+
                                 [*AV translates as 'scattereth';
                                 +AV translates as 'fan']

Wolf, Wolves   i.   A METAPHOR and SIMILE for
                            those people (and, in the case of
                            Isa.11:6, animals) who are
                            ravenous and fierce by nature.
                            Gen.49:27; Isa.11:6; 65:25;
                            Ezek.22:27; Hab.1:8

                    ii.   A SYMBOL for false religious
                            teachers who are really selfish and
                            destructive in their motives.
                            Matt.7:15; 10:16; Lk.10:3;
                            Jn.10:12; Acts 20:29

Word   A METAPHOR used as one of the titles
                                 of the Lord Jesus Christ. Just as words
                                 give us information about things, so
                                 Jesus shows us clearly what God is really
                                 like. We might say that in Christ God
                                 expressed himself. However, the
                                 Hebrew background to the title is active
                                 (see, for example, Ps.33:6) so that we
                                 should more fully say that in Christ God
                                 expressed himself, especially in terms of
                                 creation, revelation and salvation.
                                 Jn.1:1,14; 1 Jn.1:1; Rev.19:13

World(s)(ly)

i. A SYMBOL for all the people of the world including every single individual, sometimes for every human being who ever has or ever will live.
Gen.11:1*; 1 Sam.17:46*; Ps.9:8; 33:8*; 49:1; 96:13; 98:9; Isa.12:5*; 14:9*; 24:4; 26:9,18; 34:1; 40:23*; Nah.1:5; Zech.1:11*; 6:5*; Matt.13:38; 18:7; Rom.5:12,13; Rev.3:10
[*AV translates as 'earth']

ii. A SYMBOL for people representing all races, nationalities, classes, etc.
Ex.34:10*; 1 Ki.8:53*; 2 Chr.32:19*; Isa.27:6; Ezek.20:32+; Jn.4:42; 6:51; Rom.11:12,15; 2 Cor.5:19; 1 Jn.2:2; 4:9,14
[*AV translates as 'earth''; +AV translates as 'countries']

iii. A SYMBOL for the human race as a whole, although not including every single individual. In John's Gospel in particular, the emphasis is on the lostness and even the antagonism towards God, of the human race; the term 'world' has to do with quality rather than quantity (see also v.)
Matt.5:14; 26:13; Mk.14:9; 16:15; Lk.21:26*; Jn.1:9,10,29; 3:16,17,19; 6:33; 8:12,26; 9:5,39; 11:9; 12:46,47; 17:21,23; 18:20; 1 Cor.1:27,28; 2 Cor.1:12; 1 Tim.3:16; Jas.2:5; 2 Pet.2:5; 3:6
[*AV translates as 'earth']

iv.   A SYNECDOCHE for a large
majority of people or for the most
significant part of the world's
population known to the writer at
the time.
Gen.41:57*; 1 Ki.10:24+;
Isa.14:17,26+; 18:3; Lam.4:12;
Dan.4:1+;
Lk.2:1; Jn.7:4; 12:19;
Acts 17:6; 19:27; 24:5;
Rom.1:8; 1 Cor.4:9,13; Col.1:6
[*AV translates as 'lands';
+AV translates as 'earth']

v.   A SYMBOL for mankind as it is
under the power of sin and Satan
and hostile to God.
Ps.17:14; Isa.13:11; Zeph.3:8*;
Matt.4:8; Lk.4:5; 12:30; 16:8;
Jn.7:7; 8:23; 12:31; 14:17,19,
22-31; 15:18,19; 16:8,11,
20,33(b); 17:6,9,11,14-18,25;
Acts 17:31; Rom.3:6,19; 12:2;
1 Cor.1:20,21; 2:12; 3:19; 4:13;
5:10; 6:2; 11:32; 2 Cor.10:2-4+;
11:18+; Gal.3:22**; 4:3; 6:14;
Eph.2:2,12; 6:12; Col.2:8,20;
Heb.11:7,38; Jas.1:27; 4:4; 1
Pet.1:1[NIV only];2:11[NIV
only]; 5:9; 2 Pet.1:4; 2:20; 1
Jn.3:1,13; 4:1-5; 5:4,5,19; 2 Jn.7;
Rev.12:9; 13:3; 16:14; 18:23*;
[*AV translates as 'earth';
+AV translates as 'flesh';
**AV translates as 'all']

vi.   A SYMBOL for the material
possessions, the cares and

pleasures of this life, excessive attachment to these things being sinful and a snare we are warned to avoid.

Matt.16:26; Mk.8:36; Lk.9:25; 16:9*,11*; 1 Cor.7:33,34; 2 Tim.4:10; 1 Jn.2:15-17

[*AV translates as 'mammon']

vii.   A SYMBOL for this present life in contrast with heaven or hell or the world to come.

Isa.38:11

Jn.6:14; 10:36; 11:27; 12:25; 13:1; 16:21,33(b); 17:13; 18:36,37; 1 Cor.7:31; 1 Tim.1:15; 6:7,17; Heb.1:6; 10:5; 1 Jn.4:17; Rev.11:15

viii.   A METAPHOR for the earth as it will be renewed by God after the judgment and the dissolution of the present earth.

Rom.4:13; Heb.2:5

ix.   The term 'ends of the world' is a METAPHOR for everywhere in the whole earth.

Ps.19:4

Rom.10:18

x.   A METONYMY for a whole vast and complex subject. In this case, sinful human speech.

Jas.3:6

Worm(s)   i.   A METONYMY for corruption and decay of the body which in turn is a METAPHOR for the eternal pains and torments of hell.

Job 7:5; 17:14; 21:26; 24:20;
Isa.14:11; 51:8; 66:24;
Mk.9:48

ii.   A METAPHOR for one who is in
         a relatively weak and pathetic
         condition.
         Job 25:6; Ps.22:6; Isa.41:14

Wormwood   Λ METAPHOR for the bitter results of
                  sin, often as a judgment from God.
                  (Wormwood is a plant with a strong bitter
                  taste).
                  Deut.29:18*; Pro.5:4*; Jer.9:15*;
                  23:15*; Lam.3:15,19*; Amos 5:7*;
                  Rev.8:11
                  [*NIV translates as 'bitter[ness]']

Wound(s)(ed)   i.   A METAPHOR used to describe
                          the pains of conscience, or
                          sometimes for words that awaken
                          the conscience.
                          Ps.109:22; Pro.27:6; Jer.6:14*;
                          8:11*,22+;
                          1 Cor.8:12
                          [*AV translates as 'hurt';
                          +AV translates as 'health']

                  ii.   A   METAPHOR   or
                          SYNECDOCHE for afflictions,
                          often as judgments of God upon
                          sinners. With reference to Christ's
                          sufferings these are, of course,
                          inflicted upon him as he is the
                          substitute for sinners.
                          Deut.32:39; Isa.1:6; 30:26;
                          53:5; Jer.10:19; 14:17*; 15:18;
                          30:12,15+,17; 49:17**; 50:13**;
                          Lam.2:13++; Hos.6:1[NIV only];
                          Mic.1:9; Nah.3:19; Zech.13:6;
                          1 Pet.2:24*+; Rev.13:3,12,14

[*AV translates as 'blow';
+AV translates as 'affliction';
**AV translates as 'plagues';
++AV translates as 'breach'
*+AV translates as 'stripes']

Yeast   See under 'Leaven'.

Yoke   i.   A METAPHOR for slavery or for work that is very hard and demanding. This may be a result of God's judgment on sinners. It is intended by God to be seen as a picture of fallen people's slavery to sin and thus for us to seek the true freedom that comes through faith in Christ alone.
Ex.6:6*,7*; Lev.26:13; Deut.28:48; 1 Ki.12:12-14; Isa.9:4; 10:27; 14:25; 47:6; 58:6,9; Jer.2:20; 27:2-12; 28:2-14; 30:8; Lam.1:14; 3:27; Ezek.30:18; 34:27; Hos.10:11+; 11:4
Acts 15:10; Gal.5:1; 1 Tim.6:1
[*AV translates as 'burdens';
+AV translates as 'passed over']

              ii.   A METAPHOR for true believers' service to the Lord, which is a joy and a delight due to their love for Christ, but which hypocrites find burdensome.
Jer.5:5
Matt.11:29,30

Yoked   A METAPHOR for a close relationship or agreement. In these instances they involve God's people in sinful compromises.

Ps.106:28*;
2 Cor.6:14
[*AV translates as 'joined']

Yoke-fellow

A METAPHOR for a fellow believer who also labours in the service of Christ. Phil.4:3

Zion

A SYMBOL for God's dwelling-place, or for the people of God, i.e. the people among whom God dwells. This was Israel under the old covenant and they TYPIFIED the church under the new covenant. (Zion is one of the historical names for Jerusalem and was probably the name of the hill on which the original citadel stood.)
See also under 'Israel' and 'Jerusalem'.
1 Ki.8:1; 2 Ki.19:21; Ps.2:6;
Isa.1:8; Jer.3:14; Lam.1:4;
Joel 2:1; Amos 1:2; Ob.17;
Mic.1:13; Zeph.3:14; Zech.1:14;
Matt.21:5; Jn.12:15; Rom.9:33;
11:26; Heb.12:22; 1 Pet.2:6;
Rev.14:1, etc.